Warriors of Legend

Reflections of Japan in Sailor Moon (Unauthorized)

Jay Navok
and
Sushil K. Rudranath

Edited by Jonathan Mays

Cartography: Hans Schumacher
Translation aid: Bruce Clark, Andrew Floyd
Photographs: Yosenex Orengo
Additional photographs: Hans Schumacher

Third Edition, Copyright © September 2006
Genvid LLC

Published by BookSurge, LLC
North Charleston, South Carolina

Library of Congress Control Number: 2005903976
ISBN 1-4196-0814-2

Dedicated In Loving Memory to:

Rudra Nath
Teacher, Father, Friend

Violet Murad
Who Inspired a Love of Learning

Contents

Introduction

Who Are These Warriors of Legend?

A single moment can drastically change the course of a person's life. For Naoko Takeuchi, creator of the *Sailor Moon* manga series, that moment came some fifteen years ago. Her editor suggested that she create a super hero whose costume consisted of the so-called "sailor" uniforms that most Japanese schoolgirls wear to class each day. A decade and a half later, her creation has evolved across multiple media formats and earned millions of dollars. Takeuchi's vivid imagination and knack for storytelling drew her audience into the storylines and made her characters come to life. It was a success story that took place not only in Takeuchi's home of Japan, but across the globe, as the series stormed the children's TV rating charts of every country in which it aired.

The success of *Sailor Moon* can be attributed to the memorable characters and exciting plotlines written by Takeuchi, but *Sailor Moon*'s Japanese origin has been a critical component of the series' development. While *Sailor Moon* deals with universal themes like love, friendship, loyalty, and courage, it also reflects the realities of today's Japan. Even its name—based on the standard school suit that Japanese girls wear—is a Japanese cultural anecdote.

Sailor Moon thus tells two tales. One is the overt, obvious narrative of a battle between good and evil. The other is a quieter, more subtle tale, resting in subtext and implication. This second story is not a true "story" in the sense of having a definitive beginning, middle, and end. Rather, it is a series of background details that weave together the lives of the main characters into a mosaic tapestry. This tapestry illuminates the real, modern day Japan in which they live, in a way that stories set in fantastic environments cannot. This work, *Warriors of Legend*, is the analysis of that reflective mosaic.

While the magical alter egos and artifices of the "sailor soldiers" serve the overarching plot and obviously have little grounding in physical reality, the main characters remain very relatable, ordinary teenage girls. As a result, this series made for young girls doubles as a window into the nature of Japanese society.

Little details, added to make the characters' lives more realistic and relatable, are generally glossed over by the native Japanese population—after all, it is a part of their daily lives too. Consider the character Ami (Sailor Mercury), who attends an after-hours cram school. Americans may wonder why it is she has to attend more school, given how smart she is. But Japanese viewers would likely be taken by surprise if she did not go to cram school.

For native Japanese, *Sailor Moon* is more or less just another form of entertainment. Aside from the fictional plotline, there is little new there for them to see.

However, for outsiders to the culture, *Sailor Moon* provides a valuable glimpse into the workings of a society that is at turns familiar and foreign. Through the quiet trials and tribulations of characters like Ami, we see how typical girls in Japanese society live. The sailor soldiers' magical battles and titanic struggles to save the world are juxtaposed over the everyday problems of life, the latter of which are more compelling to the student of culture and humanity.

For those interested in Japan, this book, using a megahit work of Japanese cartoons/comics, serves as a fun way to learn about the country. For fans of the *Sailor Moon* series, this book will broaden their understanding of the series' underlying Japanese dynamics. And for those studying popular culture, it serves as a case study of the way in which a society is reflected therein.

But for us, *Warriors of Legend* is a tribute with gratitude to these wonderful characters and their creator, Naoko Takeuchi. They have given us so much—not the least of which is the chance to see past our own culture and journey into the land that is Japan, both as consumers of entertainment and scholars seeking enlightenment. It has been a wonderful journey for us, and we hope that for the reader, this work, *Warriors of Legend,* will prove to be just as wonderful a passport to someplace new and exciting. While *Sailor Moon* may not be as lush and lavish a production as other recent works of Japanese pop culture, such as the new *Ghost in the Shell* series, or as mind-bendingly psychoanalytical as *Evangelion*, in its own, honest and simple way, thanks to the depths of its characters and the extremely detailed nature of its contemporary surroundings, the series makes a perfect window with which to catch a glimpse of Japanese life, society, religion, and culture.

Dōmo Arigatō Gōzaimasu, Takeuchi-sensei—Thank you very much.

—Jay Navok and Sushil K. Rudranath, Esq.
May, 2005

Glossary

Because *Sailor Moon* aired in America using a different set of names from the original series, and because some reading this work may not be familiar with the show, we offer an abbreviated guide to the characters through the terms used in this book. We hope the book is broad enough that even those who are unfamiliar with the show will be able to understand how Japan is reflected in its popular culture. Characters are listed in Western style with their first names first.

Manga – Japanese word for "comics." *Sailor Moon* originally appeared as a monthly manga in the magazine *Nakayoshi* from 1992 to 1997. It ran for 52 acts consisting of five serial "arcs," as well as numerous specials.

Anime – Japanese word for "animation." *Sailor Moon* began airing as an anime shortly after it was serialized through a special package deal that Takeuchi negotiated. It ran for 200 episodes in five television "seasons," and had several films.

Sailor soldier – Our translation of the Japanese phrase *sailor senshi*, which effectively means "sailor-suited warrior." The original Japanese title of the series, *Bishōjo Senshi Sailor Moon,* was translated into English as "Pretty Soldier Sailor Moon," so we have kept the naming schematic.

Usagi Tsukino – A bubbly and energetic yet clumsy and klutzy crybaby who is the heroine of the series. She has a normal family life, with both parents and a sibling. She is also known as Sailor Moon, and is the former Princess of the Moon, Princess Serenity. She represents more or less the "normal" Japanese youth of today.

Characteristics: Usagi is the most stylized and well known of the sailor soldiers. She has blonde hair with two "dumplings or "meatballs" on the top of her head that divide her hair into two long pigtails. She is approximately fourteen years of age. In the English language series she was called "Serena."

Ami Mizuno – A shy, introverted genius girl with great skill in everything from science to chess. She lives with her mother and has only indirect contact with her estranged father. Ami comes out of her shell over the course of the series to become a well-rounded young woman. She is also known as Sailor Mercury. Her character serves as an excellent focus for issues regarding education in Japanese society.

Characteristics: Ami has short blue hair and is fourteen years old. In the English language series she was called "Amy."

Rei Hino – Rei is a Shinto *miko* (shrine maiden) with a strong personality and sense of loyalty. She is also known as Sailor Mars. Her role as a miko makes her a window into many aspects of Japanese spiritual life. Rei's character changes from manga to anime; she becomes feisty and cosmopolitan in the latter.

Characteristics: Rei has long, black hair and is fourteen years old. In the English language series she was called "Raye."

Makoto Kino – A tough tomboy whose height and power scare those around her, she has a soft caring personality within.

Makoto is the "nail that sticks out" in Japanese society. Her ostracism allows us to examine the Japanese concepts of social homogeneity and the fate of those who stand apart from the perceived societal norm. She is also known as Sailor Jupiter.

> *Characteristics:* Makoto is tall and has medium-length brown hair that is tied in a ponytail. She is fourteen years old and was called "Lita" in the English language series.

Minako Aino – Before she was Sailor Venus, the cheerful, slightly tomboyish, and somewhat lazy Minako was Sailor V, the first sailor soldier. Minako's video game-loving, idol-chasing pastimes reflect the recreational life of Japanese youth who may pursue their passions with a zest seemingly at odds with the more staid norms of Japanese culture.

> *Characteristics:* Minako has long, blonde hair. She is fourteen years old and was called "Mina" in the English language series.

Mamoru Chiba – Usagi's love interest, an elite student possessing good looks and great wealth. Also known as Tuxedo Mask and former earth royalty, Prince Endymion, the implications of his extravagant lifestyle shed light on the financial realities of what it takes to do something as simple as own a car in Japan.

> *Characteristics:* Mamoru is quite tall and has short black hair. His age depends on the series: in the manga he was in high school, in the anime he was in college. He was called "Darien" in the English language series.

Haruka Ten'ō – A suave, tough, very tomboyish junior racer and concert pianist. Her tendency to dress in men's clothing is a reference to the Japanese *takarazuka* theater revue tradition according to the author. Also known as Sailor Uranus.

> *Characteristics:* Haruka has short blonde hair and is almost as tall as Mamoru. She is in high school and was called "Amara" in the English language series.

Michiru Kaiō – The graceful, elegant counterpart to Haruka, a genius violinist also known as Sailor Neptune.

> *Characteristics:* Michiru has aqua-marine colored hair that is medium length. She is the same age as Haruka. In the English language series she was called "Michelle."

Hotaru Tomoe – A frail young girl with a tragic past steeped in death and destruction, she was featured in the third arc of *Sailor Moon*, which sheds light on Japanese syncretic attitudes towards the symbolism of foreign religions and eschatological contexts. She is also known as Sailor Saturn.

> *Characteristics:* Hotaru has short black hair. She is in middle school and was also called Hotaru in the English language series.

Chibiusa – Usagi and Mamoru's daughter from the future, also named Usagi Tsukino. (Chibiusa is a nickname, the word *chibi* being diminutive.) Known to some in the series as "Small Lady," and Sailor "Chibi Moon."

Characteristics: Chibiusa has pink hair tied in ovoid spears, reflecting differences in personality from her mother. She is in elementary school and was called "Rini" in the English language series.

Setsuna Meiō – An aloof, mysterious figure, Setsuna mainly serves as a guardian of time and a bearer of vital information. Also known as Sailor Pluto.

Characteristics: Setsuna has long, green hair and is one of the tallest sailor soldiers. Her age is unknown but physically she looks to be in her 20s. She was called "Trista" in the English language series.

Layout

This book is organized into two sections. The first explores the way the city of Tokyo has shaped the contours of *Sailor Moon.* That *Sailor Moon* takes place in Tokyo, and furthermore, in one particular ward of Tokyo, has been essential to the series' development: nearly every act of the manga or episode of the anime involves the city in some fashion.

The backdrop of Tokyo is never impartial in *Sailor Moon.* The stores in the background of a street in Takeuchi's work are not generic; they are real stores on a real street in Tokyo's Minato ward. Take, for example, the "cursed bridal shop" of the fourth manga act. This bridal shop existed in Minato at the time the series ran, and the shop's façade was the exact same as it appeared in Takeuchi's drawing. Such nuances are part of the rich fabric of the work and reflections of the real Japan that lives within it.

The city's history and experience has also made its way into *Sailor Moon*. The series occurs almost exclusively in Minato ward's Azabu-Jûban neighborhood because Takeuchi spent much of her life there, and she imparts upon the reader her own interpretation of the area through her artistry. Her staging a ghost story on Azabu's Darkness Hill was not just because the real Darkness Hill is somewhat spooky, but because ghost stories actually surround the hill in local folk legends.

We will find that even incidental backdrops are useful for understanding Tokyo's history. Depicted in an early episode of the anime is a radio station called "FM No. 10" (a pun on the name Jûban, which means "Number 10"). The building shown looks like that of Radio Japan, which existed in the same area of real Tokyo at the time. Formerly Radio Kantō, the name of the station changed to Radio Japan in the 1980s as a result of a growing listener base, and is indicative of the media trends that helped make the Tokyo dialect the national dialect.

The second half of the book explores the reflection of Japan in the series' characters. We have divided the section into five chapters, each of which is centered on a particular reflection. The first focuses on family, analyzing the nuances of Japanese families as depicted in *Sailor Moon*.

The second chapter is on culture and lifestyle, perhaps the most important aspects of Japan we can find in *Sailor Moon*. Although *Sailor Moon* has become a global phenomenon, few outside Japan are able to recognize the Japanese cultural traits that are woven into the series' fabric. The majority of children watching the show in America would not understand why the protagonist, Usagi Tsukino, bows to a telephone pole after hitting her head on it in the third episode, but instead see it as comedic and laugh. (She bowed because she bumped into someone. Bowing in apology is a Japanese cultural expression; she just didn't realize it was a pole and not a person.) An important part of *Sailor Moon*'s success has been its ability to hold those cultural attributes without affecting the appreciation of the work by those who cannot recognize them. In this chapter we will show but a few of the many Japanese cultural reflections to be found in *Sailor Moon*, attempting to understand the levels at which the series operates.

In the second chapter we will also examine daily living or lifestyle, known in Japanese as *seikatsu*. Lifestyle is an important concept to Japanese, and the understanding of lifestyle as depicted in *Sailor Moon* is one which both accents and contrasts with traditional Japanese notions of seikatsu. Characters in *Sailor Moon* follow expected Japanese norms of behavior within their lifestyle, but several have to deal with being rejected by the society they live in. We will further be examining how the life one leads, even something as simple as taking the bus versus owning a car, plays out in Japanese society, by looking at the figures involved in property ownership, education, and other aspects of life

The third chapter is on education, and is an introduction to the Japanese education system as well as how *Sailor Moon* both depicts and critiques that system. The fourth chapter is about religion. *Sailor Moon* is a series with multiple, and varied, religious connotations and reflections, and religious tradition and interpretation play a large role in what is seemingly a secular series. From Shinto shrine rituals to the use of crosses and talk of the Holy Grail, *Sailor Moon* is replete with religious symbolism. Furthermore, this symbolism is reflective of Japan's practice of syncretism—the blurring of religious distinctions—and we will examine the depiction of religious elements in *Sailor Moon* as a result of this practice.

The final chapter, foreign influences, returns to syncretism, but uses it outside of the term's normal connotation of religion. We will look at how influences from around the world, from Chinese elemental theories to Babylonian mythology, can be found in a work of Japanese fiction.

One of the most globally popular works of Japanese fiction in the recent decade, *Sailor Moon* is a series that reflects its birthplace. One of our goals in this book is not only to show this, but to examine and explicate those traits, so as to make the series accessible to all people, no matter where they live.

Thus, in the process of looking at *Sailor Moon*'s reflections of Japan, we hope to further answer the question *Who are these Warriors of Legend*?

Sailor Moon: A Primer

Who is Naoko Takeuchi?

*N*aoko Takeuchi is one of the Japanese manga industry's greatest success stories. Her franchise, *Sailor Moon*, has grossed billions worldwide, and Takeuchi's popularity in Japan and abroad is unmatched among manga artists. Although her characters' family lives are often dysfunctional, the first twenty years of Takeuchi's life were perfectly normal. She was born on March 15, 1967, in Kofu City in Yamanashi prefecture. Her parents, Kenji and Ikuko, always made time for her, and a few years later, she gained a little brother named Shingo. She and her brother both grew up in the area, remaining in Yamanashi through high school.

Takeuchi found time for both art and astronomy clubs in middle school, and she wrote several short manga stories during those years. Almost every Japanese child dreams of becoming a manga artist at one time or another, so Takeuchi's interest was not unusual. It was in high school that Takeuchi took her manga stories more seriously. She sketched constantly—when it did not get in the way of her math and science studies. At the age of eighteen, Takeuchi penned *It's Not a Dream, Right?*, which she would later publish as part of the two-volume *Prism Time* series.

After she completed *It's Not a Dream, Right?*, Takeuchi was still unsure of becoming a professional manga artist, and instead pursued a degree in chemistry. She spent the next several years at Kyoritsu Chemical University and Kyoritsu Institute of Pharmacy, balancing her time between manga serials and a thesis on "The Heightened Effects of

Thrombolytic Actions Due to Ultrasound."

Takeuchi, while still a university student, made her manga artist debut with "Love Call" in the September 1986 issue of *Nakayoshi Deluxe*, a comic serial. The manga earned her Nakayoshi's New Manga Artist Award. Takeuchi was thrilled, not only because Nakayoshi was a national publication and a perfect venue for her to launch a career, but also because it was her favorite childhood magazine and a gateway to the world of girl's manga.

Takeuchi continued her studies, and, three years later, was employed at Keiō Hospital. Takeuchi was living a double life: pharmacist by day, manga artist by night. She managed to continue this for sixteen months. In late 1990, Takeuchi quit her day job and decided to focus on manga full time.

In October of 1990, Takeuchi began her first major manga series, called *The Cherry Project*. The three-volume series wrapped up in December 1991. After a well deserved break, Takeuchi and her editor, Fumio Osano (better known as "Osa-P," a joke used in the *Sailor Moon* series), decided that her next project would be a "magical girl fighting for love and justice." After a suggestion that the heroine wear a "sailor suit" like most young schoolgirls in Japan, the result was *Code Name: Sailor V*. It was published on July 18, 1991, in the Summer issue of a Nakayoshi companion magazine, *Runrun*.

Sailor V performed well, and, together with Takeuchi's manga publisher, Kodansha, a deal was struck to create a "mixed media" franchise, releasing a new manga and anime series simultaneously. The series was planned as *Pretty Soldier Sailor V*. But, before production began, Takeuchi and Osa-P decided to adapt the popular five-person team style instead, shifting the focus from Sailor V to a new title lead, "Sailor Moon." After a few more adjustments to the storyline, the *Pretty Soldier Sailor Moon* manga began its run in 1992, followed by the anime's premiere shortly thereafter. All the pieces were in place for *Sailor Moon* to be a hit, but Takeuchi was not expecting the success it eventually gained, so she only prepared a story for the first season.

The *Sailor Moon* anime did not stop at one season. But that led to a problem: the anime was moving more quickly than the manga. Instead of waiting for Takeuchi to provide more stories, the animators created their own for the first thirteen episodes of the second season. It was just one in a number of moves that displeased Takeuchi, but she was so busy writing the show that she had no time to worry about it then. At one point, her monthly workload included:

- 40-50 page serial with 10 color pages
- Two special edition books
- 64-page "special issue" supplement
- 135-page trade paperback
- Outlines for anime episodes
- Appointments and data collection

Takeuchi eventually came to the verge of total collapse. One day, when she and her editor were discussing a disagreement, she let him have it:

> —*I'm done. I'll not draw any more!*
> —*What of the magazines that are waiting for your manga? And the animation series?*
> —*I'm going crazy! I'm stopping everything, I can't continue!*[1]

Osa-P, seeing the enormously successful franchise beginning to crumble from within, tried everything to persuade her to continue. Longer breaks? A little less work? Abandoning that

Sailor V manga that still hung over her? It seemed nothing would convince Takeuchi to draw even one more frame.

Annoyed and terrified, Osa-P tried one more time:

—And your readers?

Takeuchi paused for a moment. What about those readers, those hundreds of thousands who wait impatiently for the next chapter of her story? If she dropped everything in progress, how would they feel? Crushed, angry, betrayed. She simply couldn't do it to her fans.

—For them, I must continue.

It was not about contracts or financial commitments or even professionalism—Takeuchi was close to throwing everything out the window just to preserve her sanity. But thanks to a plea from a desperate editor, she held herself together until the end.

The fifth and final season of the *Sailor Moon* anime came to a close on February 7, 1997, and the *Sailor Moon* and *Sailor V* manga series wrapped up one and three months later, respectively. Takeuchi had survived, but, for a period of half a decade, the daily demands of the manga industry had run her ragged. She was constantly sick, and Japan's disparate weather did not treat her allergies kindly.

Although she gained a brief vacation, the demands of the industry called her back to establish a new series. She would eventually have a fight with her publisher, Kodansha, and work for a different manga company; starting and stopping series, unable to focus for a period of a half decade.

In 2003, a new *Sailor Moon* series began airing on Japanese television. This version featured real actors and actresses, and, although it did not reach the fame of its animated predecessor, performed very well for its time slot. At the same time the new series was airing, Takeuchi revised the entire *Sailor V* and *Sailor Moon* manga canon, "updating it for the 21st century." With the last volumes released in fall of 2004, *Sailor Moon*'s millennial revival ended as well.

Takeuchi now lives with her husband, also a famous manga artist named Yoshihiro Togashi (writer of the series *Yu Yu Hakusho*, which airs currently on American television) and her son.

What is the story of Sailor Moon?

10,000 years ago, both the earth and the moon housed great civilizations. The Moon Kingdom (known as the *Silver Millennium*) oversaw the development of the primitive humans on the planet earth. The humans, for their part, longed for and resented the immortality of those on the moon. A malevolent force known as Metallia made good use of the simmering human hatreds, corrupting them and creating a "Dark Kingdom" whose forces plunged the two spheres into war.

Queen Serenity, the ruler of the Moon Kingdom, watched in horror as her four guardians, the "sailor soldiers" Sailor Mercury, Sailor Mars, Sailor Jupiter, and Sailor Venus, fell before the advancing enemy. The Queen was crushed to see her daughter, Princess Serenity—and Princess Serenity's lover, the Prince of the Earth, Endymion—killed. Serenity had a choice to make. Obliterate the enemy here, for all time, and consign the souls of her protectors and her daughter to oblivion forever, or seal the enemy and allow the souls of those she loved to be reborn on the earth at some point in the future. She chose the latter option, dying in the process but believing that the sailor soldiers and her daughter could have happy lives in the future—but aware that should the evil reawaken once more, they would have to take up the battle in her stead.

In the present day, the evil has awakened again, and the warriors who had fought that forgotten war have been reborn in Tokyo, Japan. So begins the story of *Sailor Moon.*

The first of the sailor soldiers to reawaken, Minako Aino, is a typical teenage girl more interested in going out on dates or sneaking into pop concerts than fighting for justice. But thanks to a magical pen given to her by a talking cat named Artemis—one of the few survivors from the long-forgotten battle of the past—she is able to unlock the power that is her birthright—the power of Sailor Venus.

The *Sailor V* manga (the beginning of the *Sailor Moon* plotline) follows Sailor Venus, who, knowing herself only to be the "idol soldier" Sailor V, battles the forces of the mysterious "Dark Agency"—an organization dedicated to manipulating pop stars and idols (young singers/models) in order to extract the energy of Japanese teens for their own nefarious purposes. At first, the Agency is perceived as a mere petty threat, but Takeuchi reveals it to be a front for the reawakened Dark Kingdom. With the stakes raised, and the great war of the past threatening to engulf the world of today, the *Sailor V* manga ends with Sailor V regaining all the memories of her past life and embracing her true destiny as Sailor Venus, who would be introduced in the *Sailor Moon* manga.

As the *Sailor Moon* manga (and anime) opens, Sailor V's legend has spread across Japan, making quite an impression on a klutzy girl named Usagi Tsukino. This most unheroic young lady runs into a talking cat named Luna. Like Minako before her, she too becomes a sailor soldier, Sailor Moon, through the help of a magical brooch.

Usagi muddles her way through her first few battles with the help of Luna and a dashing, mysterious figure known as Tuxedo Mask (by night, and Mamoru Chiba by day). Being a soldier of "love and justice" is not a job Usagi wants, and, as the Dark Kingdom's minions continue to wreak havoc across the city, Usagi fears she will have to shoulder the burden of battle alone. Fortunately for her, help arrives in the form of the shy genius, Ami Mizuno.

Ami, unlike the playful and somewhat irresponsible Usagi, is a dedicated student who takes study very seriously. Like a typical Japanese student, she lives a life split between regular school and an after-hours cram school. When the Dark Kingdom exploits the Japanese cram school industry in an attempt to harvest the energy of the nation's overstressed students, the process nearly takes Ami's life. This assault causes Ami to awaken as the soldier of wisdom, Sailor Mercury.

If Ami Mizuno is a nod to the contemporary mold of Japanese society, then the next soldier to awaken, Rei Hino, is a product of its history. An aloof and mysterious *miko* (Shrine maiden), she joins the group when a Dark Kingdom plot implicates her in a series of odd kidnappings. Rei has to use her traditional powers to divine the truth of the matter, and, in doing so, comes face to face with her destiny as the soldier of flame, Sailor Mars.

Where Ami and Rei's personalities exemplify two facets of "normal" Japanese society, the next sailor soldier—Makoto Kino, a.k.a. Sailor Jupiter—is typical of the nonconformist "nail that sticks out." Taller and stronger than other girls her age, she is an anomaly in a culture that claims homogeneity. Ostracized and feared by her peers, she had resigned herself to a life of solitude—a life that Usagi rescues her from.

Together, the four girls seek the reincarnated Princess Serenity, the one person capable of defeating the Dark Kingdom and preventing the tragedy of the past from occurring once again. It is at this time that Minako Aino reappears, shedding her guise as Sailor V and assuming her true identity as Sailor Venus. She also claims to be the legendary princess. The "Sailor Team" is complete, and the girls who become known as the "five guardians" of Tokyo's Azabu-Jûban town take their place in legend.

Sailor Venus' role as princess was merely that of decoy, however, and the real princess eventually emerges—none other than Usagi herself. She is Princess Serenity of the Silver Millennium, and Mamoru Chiba, who had been protecting her as Tuxedo Mask, is Prince Endymion of ten millennia prior.

Unsure of herself and her new power, Usagi does her best to continue living her life normally. The past is not something she wanted to dwell on. But when the Dark Kingdom kidnaps the man she is becoming fond of—Mamoru Chiba—she and the others hunt the Dark Kingdom down to their lair in the North Pole in order to save him and bring peace to the world.

In an episode with immense impact upon its young viewers, the sailor soldiers fall in battle, one after the other. Children across Japan were mortified as their heroines—their friends—whom they had followed for over a year—were abruptly executed, leaving Usagi to face the leader of the Dark Kingdom, Queen Beryl, all by herself.

Usagi prevails, and uses her powers to revive her friends and stop the Dark Kingdom forever. Initially, the series was to end at this point—but its phenomenal popularity ensured a second season would be in the works.

The popularity of the animated show caught both Takeuchi and the animators by surprise. Takeuchi did not have enough time to write a new storyline before the deadline for writing new animation episodes could be met. The animators decided to write a storyline of their own. The first batch of episodes are a self-contained plot concerning a *makaijû* (demon tree) and the efforts of two villains, Ail and Ann, who go to extreme lengths to keep it alive. These episodes are significant in that they are a wholly unique take on the *Sailor Moon* universe on the part of the animation staff, and so do not necessarily reflect Naoko Takeuchi's thematic vision, but do reflect the anime writers' own understanding of the series and Tokyo.

The second part of the second anime season, which correlates to the second manga arc, introduces a "Crystal

Tokyo" of 1,000 years in the future, a utopian city founded by Usagi following twentieth century Tokyo's apparent annihilation. Due to events never fully explained in the series, the earth has suffered a massive natural disaster, and Usagi assumes the reigns of power as Neo-Queen Serenity.

A separatist faction known as the Black Moon leaves earth rather than remain subject to Serenity's rule, and they exile themselves to the planet Nemesis. There, a malevolent being known as "Wise Man" convinces them to launch an attack on the Tokyo of the past in order to prevent the founding of Crystal Tokyo. To do this, they attack strategic "crystal points" located in Azabu-Jûban, which form the foundation of the pentagram shaped Crystal Palace fortress.

The Black Moon is not alone in their attempt to change the past. A small girl bravely makes her way into the past, seeking the power of Usagi's brooch and the help of the legendary sailor soldier, Sailor Moon. She is the future daughter of Usagi and Mamoru, nicknamed "Chibiusa" (Small Usagi). With Chibiusa's help, the future earth is saved, and the sailor soldiers make a new friend.

The third season of the anime continues the realism of the first two, with many of the central locales based on real-life structures. Story-wise, the issues presented are more complex. Whereas previously Usagi and friends are able to win their battles through "the power of love" or "friendship," in this season the stakes are considerably higher.

The enemy, known as the "Death Busters," seek three mystical talismans—a sword, a mirror and a jewel akin to three mythical Japanese treasures called the *Shinki*—that are sealed within the pure hearts of human beings. The removal of those talismans means certain death for their carrier. While Usagi and company are unwilling to allow three innocents to die, two new sailor soldiers appear—and they are far more amenable to the notion of sacrificing the lives of the innocent in order to save the world.

Sailors Uranus and Neptune—Haruka Ten'ō and Michiru Kaiō, respectively—are older than the others. They are pragmatic about their duties, willing to "dirty their hands" in order to make sure the mission gets accomplished. The bulk of the season sees them clashing both physically and philosophically with Usagi's "Sailor Team" in a battle that is as much a quest for ideological supremacy as it is battlefield superiority.

The final sailor soldier to appear, the young and frail Hotaru Tomoe, represents the ultimate expression of this conflict, taken from abstract ideas about the needs of the many and the few. As Sailor Saturn, her role is to cleanse the world of evil by destroying it. Haruka and Michiru decide that, in order to save the world, they will take preemptive action and snuff out her life before she can awaken to her powers. Usagi and the others are appalled, and do their best to save Hotaru. In the end, Hotaru sacrifices herself, and is reborn.

Sailor Moon continued for two more storylines. Although they too have reflections of Japan, by the end of the third storyline all the sailor soldiers were introduced and commentary on much of Japanese society already dealt with. The latter seasons relied upon the fantasy elements of the series (a mythical unicorn who lived in dreams, and a war between the sailor soldiers) to drive their plot. We will not be covering them in any detail in this book.

Exploring the *Sailor Moon* Universe

"We were born on this small planet called "earth."
Each of us may only be a tiny, powerless life force,
But we want to enjoy our short lives as much as we can."
— Sailor Moon, Second Film

*T*he heroine of our series, Usagi Tsukino, may be the savior of the earth, but her heroics are confined to her immediate vicinity—the city of Tokyo, Japan. Considering the amount of dangerous activity that takes place in her proximity, perhaps it is just as well for the rest of the world's inhabitants that this is the case.

The sailor soldiers' battles in Tokyo are numerous and legendary. What many may not realize is that, far from being set in some fictional wards and locales of the city, many of the battlegrounds and background scenery depicted in the various iterations of the *Sailor Moon* universe do in fact exist in Tokyo (or did when the manga and anime were current), albeit usually with their names modified for copyright reasons.

Foreign fans of *Sailor Moon* may perceive the backdrop of the series as nothing more than an abstract urban setting. But because many of the locations featured in the anime and manga did exist in reality, Japanese fans would have had a far more thrilling experience as they recognized famous landmarks and locations; building the notion that the sailor soldiers could have easily walked alongside them in their travels through Tokyo.

Here we hope to bring some of that wonder and excitement to fans of *Sailor Moon* unfamiliar with the geography and history of Tokyo, as we examine "where worlds collide"—walking where Sailor Moon and her friends have walked, and stepping, for a time, into the culture and history of their world—and another part of our own.

Before we can begin to examine Sailor Moon's travels through Tokyo, it is necessary to understand a bit about the way the city itself is laid out.

Sailor Moon's home city of Tokyo is divided into numerous wards, rather like the "boroughs" of New York City—except there are 23 of them. Tokyo is a massive city, encompassing not only the urban environment most associated with it, but also an expanding suburban sector, and even rural farmlands and islands. Each of Tokyo's wards is further divided into districts, then sub-districts, and finally "chōme" and "banchi." (The latter are used to derive the exact addresses of locations, as the Japanese do not use the same address system employed in the West.)

Located in the southeastern section of Tokyo and facing Tokyo Bay to the east is Minato ward, where we will be focusing much of our attention, as most of the series is staged there. Adjoining it are Shinjuku and Chiyoda wards to the north, Shibuya ward to the west, and Shinagawa ward to the south. In its entirety, Minato ward is not large: at 3.3% of the total land area of Tokyo's 23 wards, it is about the size of Manhattan.[2]

Minato ward contains a lot of places that those who are at least casually familiar with Tokyo may have heard of, such as Roppongi—a famous "red light" district. It is also the setting of many events and destinations associated with the city, like the Tokyo Tower.

The ward is not crowded for Tokyo: it has about 160,000 registered residents (with a relatively large percentage of that, 15,000, being foreigners). According to registered resident statistics from the ward's town hall, Minato ward is

The eastern half of Tokyo.

one of the *least* dense wards in Tokyo, ranking 21st out of the 23 wards, yet the daytime population of the ward is over 850,000 people.[3]

Why the disparity? Minato ward is one of the centers of what is called the "doughnut effect," whereby the number of people there in the day and the number at night (the number of people who actually *live* there) are vastly different. This is an ever more common feature in the eastern part of Tokyo where Minato is located; most people do not want to live in the ward (which is very expensive) and would rather commute to it.

Many people pack into Tokyo's subway trains every day. They are commuting to wards like Minato. Furthermore, the eastern wards are facing a steadily declining population. This may explain why, despite the series occurring in Tokyo— one of the most crowded cities in the world—we often see streets quiet and empty at night in *Sailor Moon*.

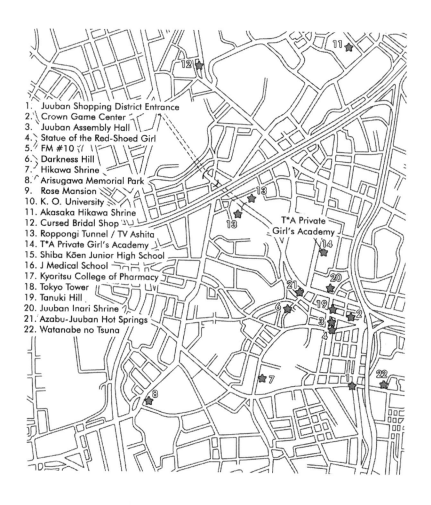

1. Juuban Shopping District Entrance
2. Crown Game Center
3. Juuban Assembly Hall
4. Statue of the Red-Shoed Girl
5. FM #10
6. Darkness Hill
7. Hikawa Shrine
8. Arisugawa Memorial Park
9. Rose Mansion
10. K. O. University
11. Akasaka Hikawa Shrine
12. Cursed Bridal Shop
13. Roppongi Tunnel / TV Ashita
14. T*A Private Girl's Academy
15. Shiba Kōen Junior High School
16. J Medical School
17. Kyoritsu College of Pharmacy
18. Tokyo Tower
19. Tanuki Hill
20. Juuban Inari Shrine
21. Azabu-Juuban Hot Springs
22. Watanabe no Tsuna

T*A Private
Girl's Academy

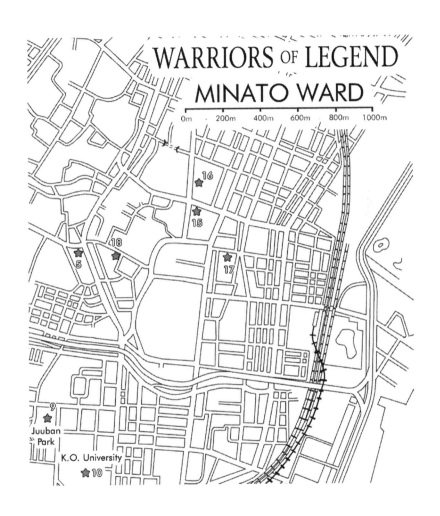

WARRIORS OF LEGEND
MINATO WARD

0m · 200m · 400m · 600m · 800m · 1000m

Juuban Park

K.O. University

Azabu

While Minato ward is a small part of Tokyo, most of the events that occur in *Sailor Moon* do so in a single district of the ward: Azabu-Jûban. Only a couple of square kilometers in area, Azabu-Jûban is the place most of the sailor soldiers call home. With so much happening in such a small area, it is no wonder they are constantly running into each other—and trouble.

The naming convention behind Azabu-Jûban is interesting. In North America, we tend to name places after what the Native Americans had called them (like "Manhattan" or "Toronto") or after the areas that the colonizers came from ("New York" or "British Columbia"). The Japanese tend to name areas by their geography. Most of modern Tokyo was farmland or fields just a few centuries ago, and the names tend to reflect that. Azabu, for example, comes from "free-flowing hemp": *asa* is "hemp" which used to *fu-eru*, that is, to increase or grow plentifully. Jûban's name is even more blunt: *Jûban* means "Number 10," so Azabu-Jûban (the full name of the town) means "Azabu Number 10." It was given the name because when the banks of the local river, the *Furukawa*, were strengthened in 1675, the river was split up into sections, and Jûban was the tenth section. Jokes and references to the Jûban naming convention are made throughout the series, and we will investigate them as we go along.

Another notable aspect of Azabu is its concentration of foreign embassies; most of the foreign embassies in Japan are crowded into this one area.

When Japan first opened its doors to the outside world in the late 1850s, Azabu's location—the port of Tokyo bay—made it quite appropriate for foreign consulates. American legate Townsend Harris moved there in 1859, and although the embassy is now in nearby Akasaka, many other countries followed his lead. This may be why royalty are depicted several times in *Sailor Moon* as living in this part of Tokyo.[4]

Rainbow Bridge
Shibaura, Minato ward

Completed just as the second season of the *Sailor Moon* anime began airing was one of Minato ward's most famous new symbols, the Rainbow Bridge. It is a suspension bridge that extends over the Tokyo Port and is located in northern Tokyo Bay. Built to relieve Tokyo traffic, Rainbow Bridge opened on August 26, 1993, and connects Shibaura Wharf (and a new development on the waterfront) with a location called Odaiba in Minato ward. The bridge is referred to as Tokyo Bay's "new symbol" and is 1870 feet long. Three lines of transportation go across the bridge: on top is the Metropolitan Express No. 11 highway, and on the lower deck the *Yurikamome* New Transit routes run.

Although the structure is called the "Rainbow Bridge," the towers are white, painted to match the skyline of central Tokyo. The rainbow aspect of the name comes from how the bridge looks when it is lit up at night. Lamps have been placed on the wires supporting the bridge and they illuminate red, white, and green every night—powered by solar cells on the bridge itself. The ward office says that this gives the bridge a "magical effect."

The animators

used this new landmark to their advantage and featured it in the series. It is highlighted in the show's second season opening sequence, with protagonist Usagi Tsukino peering out at it on a dark, cold Tokyo night.

Azabu-Jûban Entrance

Anthropological studies of Tokyo, like Theodore Bestor's *Neighborhood Tokyo*, often highlight an interesting feature of Tokyo's neighborhoods: they tend to revolve around their shopping districts. In some of the smaller Tokyo neighborhoods, these shopping districts are single streets where almost all of the town's business is conducted.[5]

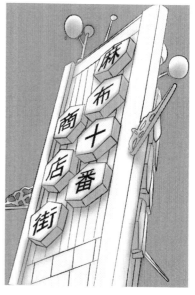

With this in mind, it is no surprise that *Sailor Moon*'s Azabu-Jûban is centered around its shopping district. Its entrance sign is shown often in the series and has become one of *Sailor Moon*'s most distinctive background images.

The large sign is reminiscent of something found in New York's Times Square, and is advertising the Jûban neighborhood. The text on the full sign, apart from saying "Jûban Shopping Center," also declares that Azabu-Jûban is the "town of smiles." Unfortunately the sign has long since been taken down, but the Azabu-Jûban entrance sign lives on in the hearts of *Sailor Moon* fans as a symbol of that place which the sailor soldiers call home.

Crown Pachinko

Featured as the "Crown Game Parlor" in both the *Sailor Moon* anime and manga, this site is a focal point for the series. Usagi often takes her friends here when she first meets them, as a sort of ice-breaker.

Although it no longer exists, the real Crown center, whose outward appearance was nearly identical to what was shown in the anime, was called "Crown Pachinko." Pachinko is a mixture between slot machines and pinball in which the player is quite passive, controlling only the speed with which many small steel balls are thrown into the pachinko machine. They are usually smoky and noisy places and a bit boring for girls Usagi's age.

Located near Crown Pachinko's real-life location is a store called "Jewel A." Jewel A is the real-life counterpart building to the fictional jewelry store featured in the first episode of *Sailor Moon* and owned by the mother of Usagi's friend, Naru Osaka. It is called "Jewelry OSA-P" in the series.

How did this unusual name for a jewelry store come about? Naoko Takeuchi used her editor's nickname (Osa-P) and combined it with the name "Jewel A." Adding "P" to the end of one's name is a common way to make a nick-name in Japan. For example, Minako Aino (Sailor Venus) was often called "Mina-P."

Azabu-Jûban Assembly Hall

In an early episode of the *Sailor Moon* anime, Shinto shrine maiden Rei Hino (Sailor Mars) uses her spiritual powers to cheat and win a Japanese lottery contest. In the game, a large wheel is spun and a colored ball comes out of the machine. This type of lottery is called *Chûsen* and shopkeepers typically run a Chûsen lottery as a gimmick in order to attract customers.

When a customer makes a purchase, he or she receives a ticket to try his or her luck at the lottery wheel. To win something, it is necessary to get the right colored ball. Often the number of times one gets to spin is dependent on the purchase, and it usually takes quite a number of spins before one wins something worthwhile. Rei probably did not purchase much, which could be why the shopkeeper is so surprised (and annoyed) when she wins on her first try.

It is not certain whether the Chûsen lottery in the series was held in front of this particular hall, called the Azabu-Jûban Assembly Hall in the real world, but many are held in front of here on a regular basis. Shopkeepers who want to run similar promotional lotteries often do them in front of the Azabu-Jûban assembly hall, since there are a lot of passers-by.[6]

This hall is also featured as the site of a wedding contest in the series, and is indeed a location where many Japanese get married. Although traditional Japanese wedding ceremonies are still conducted in Japan, characterized by kimono and sitting on one's knees, many Japanese girls prefer the Western-style wedding they see on television, replete with white gowns and tuxedo'd men. Often a compromise is necessary between whether a traditional or Western-style wedding will be held, and sometimes the couple has both in succession so as to appease the husband (who may want the Japanese-style wedding) and the wife (who desires her dreamy Western-style wedding).

Statue of the Girl in Red Shoes

In a memorable episode of the third season of the *Sailor Moon* anime, genius schoolgirl Ami Mizuno (Sailor Mercury) regains her confidence to do well in school while sitting next to this statue of a girl in red shoes named Kimi-chan.

The statue exists in Azabu-Jûban and is modeled after a real girl named Kimi-chan, who was featured in a well known children's song called "The Girl in Red Shoes." The lyric writer was a Japanese poet called Ujō Noguchi, and the musical composer was Nagayo Motōri. Motōri (1885-1945) was a descendant of Norinaga Motōri, a famous scholar of Japanese literature who studied music and composed many children's songs. Norinaga is even supposed to have composed the first Japanese children's song.

In the song "The Girl in Red Shoes" a young girl accompanies a foreigner by ship from Yokohama. The real Kimi-chan was supposed to have done the same—or so her mother thought. Kimi Iwasaki was born in Shimizu in the city of Shizuoka, on July 15, 1902. She was adopted at the age of three by American missionary Charles Huit and his wife. Kimi's mother, Kayo, had given her up for adoption to work in Hokkaido, believing she had done the best for her daughter.

But Kimi-chan had a weak constitution. She came

down with tuberculosis (which was incurable at the time) just before she was supposed to leave for America. Her adopted parents left her in a church orphanage in Azabu-Jûban, where Kimi passed away at the age of nine on September 15, 1911. The orphanage she died at was Toriizaka Church, which stood at Azabu-Nagasaka between 1877 and 1923.

Ujō Noguchi worked in the same company as Kimi's mother Kayo. Noguchi heard Kimi's story from her mother and wrote the lyrics to *Akai Kutsu* (Red Shoes). In later years, it is said that Kayo would often say, "Ujō made that song for you, Kimi," and sing, "A Little Girl Wearing Red Shoes." Her voice was full of sadness and regret.

When a Hokkaido newspaper wrote a chance story on the girl's tragic life in November 1973, her life became widely known around the country. Several statues dedicated to Kimi were erected—the one in Azabu-Jûban dates from 1989.[7]

In the episode where the statue is featured, Ami is contemplating why she works so hard at her school work and why she wants to be a doctor like her mother. As she sits next to the statue, Ami regains her confidence to continue studying for her future career. It is likely the animation staff chose this location for Ami to sit at because they wanted to emphasize Ami's feelings for her mother, whom Ami seeks to emulate. Indeed, the watercolor backgrounds that make up the *Sailor Moon* series seem to have subtle but deep meanings.

Radio Japan

Radio station FM No. 10 pops up with relative frequency in the *Sailor Moon* universe. The name is a pun on Azabu-Jûban; as we have noted, the word Jûban means Number 10. But in the *Sailor Moon* universe, that is the station's handle and not its official name—according to a ticket shown in a later episode of the anime, its official name is "Tokyo FM Broadcasting."

This official name is similar to its real-world counterpart, which exists on the same site that it did when the series was airing. Originally the real world station was called "Radio Kantō," named after the particular region of Honshu (the main Japanese island) where Tokyo is located, but the station changed its name to "Radio Japan" in the mid 1980s to reflect a larger listening base.

This change is indicative of a larger trend involving the media and the spread of the Tokyo dialect as Japan's "national dialect." Although Japan is a relatively small country about the size of California, for many centuries its rocky terrain made contact between villages difficult. All the different villages spoke Japanese, each developed a different dialect of the language, which sometimes made communication between villages difficult.

The various dialect enclaves began to gravitate toward Edo (the old name for Tokyo) when the city became the country's capital in the early seventeenth century. However, Edo's pull was not yet strong enough to make its own version of the dialect a standard, and the regional dialects remained entrenched through the mid-twentieth century.

By that time, television and radio began to have an effect on regional dialect. Because most of the media was based in Tokyo, it was natural that the Tokyo dialect became the national dialect as Tokyo's media influence grew in the post

World War II environment.

Although Tokyo dialect is what most people in Japan understand (and is what is taught in Japanese language courses in the United States) a few regional dialects have weathered the last half century. The Kansai dialect, sometimes referred to as the Osaka dialect, as well as the Okinawa dialect, are just two examples of regional dialects that have resisted the Tokyo pull enough to remain intact.

The Radio Japan building.

Darkness Hill
Azabu-Jûban

On the outskirts of Azabu-Jûban is a winding road that never seems to end, and is shrouded in mystery and ghostly legends. This road is one of Tokyo's many *saka-michi* or slopes—a defining feature of the large city. Paul Waley, a Tokyo historian, wrote the following of them:

> *Tokyo is a city of slopes: masculine slopes, feminine slopes, philosopher's slopes, fisherman's slopes, ghostly slopes, dumpling slopes, sick person's slopes, beggars' slopes, and tiptoe slopes. Most cities name all their roads, but Tokyo, at least in traditional terms, has names for only its sloping roads, its sakamichi.*

There are over five hundred named slopes in the city. Book upon book has been written on the subject of Tokyo's slopes, with long, learned discussions on whether such-and-such a slope should really be a hundred meters higher up the hill or whether a slope's name is derived from its shape or the occupation of the local inhabitants.[8]

The slope you see in the photograph is called *Kurayami zaka* in Japanese, which literally translates to "Darkness Hill." ("Hill," in this case, fits better than "slope.") It becomes the setting for a *Sailor Moon* side-story where a vampire named Lyrica Hubert takes residence in a haunted embassy at the top of the hill, one of the series' few Halloweenish episodes.

The hill can be found on the very edge of Azabu-Jûban. We mentioned before that Jûban is home to many embassies; as would be expected, there is even one here—the Austrian Embassy resides on this very hill.

In the day, Darkness Hill seems like just another desolate hill (although it is said that the trees and shrubs are dark even at noon). But there are legends surrounding the hill, including a ghost story written about a poltergeist who considered it his personal haunt. It is said that when you walk along the hill at night, you can still see the spectre of a fair-skinned man's ghost walking up and down it. How fitting that Takeuchi would seek to use the hill as a setting for her own ghoulish tale.[9]

Usually the real life and *Sailor Moon* locations match up, but in this case, there is a slight difference between the two worlds. In the *Sailor Moon* universe, the embassy is at the top of the hill, while in our world, the Austrian embassy can be found around the middle of the hill. Still, it goes to show how much detail was put into the series; there is nary a place shown that does not have a real life counterpart somewhere.

Hikawa Shrine
Moto-Azabu ("Old" Azabu)

The Azabu Hikawa Shrine is one of *Sailor Moon*'s most famous landmarks and important locations. It is the functional home turf for the girls: they study, hold meetings and in general, use it as everyone's home away from home (and in the case of Rei Hino/Sailor Mars, it is her actual home).

It is important to note, though, that there are many "Hikawa" Shinto shrines located around Japan, and there are even several in Tokyo. In the manga version of *Sailor Moon*, the exterior of the shrine shown is the same as that of Azabu's Hikawa shrine. The anime, however, uses the Hikawa shrine in Akasaka as its model, so what we see in the anime and what we see in the manga (and in real life) are actually two different shrines. We will get into the Akasaka Hikawa Shrine later; for the time being, let us investigate more about the Hikawa Shrine located in Moto-Azabu.

"Hikawa" refers to the shrine's denomination. The Azabu Hikawa shrine is the place where Rei Hino lives and spends her time as the shrine's maiden, but as we have said, it is not the only Hikawa shrine in Japan, and Hikawa is not the only type of Shinto shrine; there are many denominations.

In general, the difference in denomination between shrines has to do with the legend behind the shrine, its location, and its history. All three intertwine, making each shrine unique. Yet the Azabu Hikawa shrine was not just selected for the *Sailor Moon* series because it is in Azabu; there are actually good mythological reasons for Takeuchi's choosing of this specific shrine.

Historical background of the Hikawa Shrines

Hikawa shrines are located all around Japan, with over 200 shrines belonging to the denomination. The history of the Hikawa shrines is still debated even today because different shrines have different legends that they want to promote as the "real story" behind their birth. The most popular of the founding stories for the Azabu shrine relate to the Minamoto clan.

The Minamoto clan was one of two clans vying for control of Japan in the middle ages. The first leader of the Minamoto clan saw that a large number of imperial princes was straining the resources of the Imperial Court and decided to move east—to make things easier on the royal budget, stake his own fortune, and conquer new lands for his clan. These founding stories hold that the first of the Hikawa shrines was established under the reign of Tsunemoto Minamoto in 939 CE, or at the time of his child, Mitsunaka Minamoto's birth.

Why the name "Hikawa"?

The word "Hikawa" derives from a river in Izumo (Shimane prefecture, in western Japan) called the *Hinokawa*. (*Hi* means fire, and *kawa* means river, so the name is literally "River of Fire.") When it was named, the Hinokawa River was a reddish color, almost like the "red" iron of antique metals—this is where the "river of fire" idea originates. Although the Hikawa shrine actually writes its name with the character for "ice," the pronounciation is the same as that of the word for "fire." *Sailor Moon*, however, uses the character for fire, rather than ice, because it is more fitting for the fiery Sailor Mars, Rei Hino, who lives in the shrine.

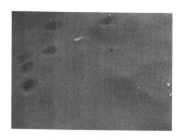

Iron Sand in the Hinokawa River area.

The Hinokawa region of Japan is famous for its ironwork—the area boasts very high-quality iron sand, which is why the river turns red. Iron is associated alchemically with the planet Mars. In addition, a very hot fire is needed to make armor from this indigenous iron, and given this, it should come as no shock that the strong-willed, fiercely loyal and indefatigable Rei Hino should have come from an environment like a Hikawa shrine.

The legendary purpose of Hikawa Shrines

Susanō no Mikoto, brother of the legendary sun goddess Amaterasu Okami, is a very important figure in Japanese mythology. He is the enshrined deity of the Azabu Hikawa Shrine and, according to legend, was responsible for saving a princess named Kushiinada by slaying an eight-headed dragon known as *Yamata no Orochi*. (Not coincidentally, this took place near the banks of the river Hinokawa.) It was in the process of saving this Princess that he obtained the three sacred treasures, known in the *Sailor Moon* universe as the three Talismans. More on the legend of Susanō and the sacred treasures will follow later in the book.

For now, note how Susanō became the Hikawa Shrine's deity. According to myth, a tribe called the Mononobe— renowned for their creation of 'serpent totems'—was expelled when a clan known as the Izumo invaded. Fearing the wrath of the enraged serpent gods, the Izumo "spread the spirit" of Susanō, the great slayer of dragons and serpents, far and wide to keep them at bay. Two hundred and twenty-seven Hikawa Shrines were established, and the vengeance of Yamata no Orochi's brethren was quelled.[10]

Prince Arisugawa Memorial Park

The Prince Arisugawa Memorial Park, considered one of the most majestic (and green) parks in Tokyo, covers an entire city block. One may think of it as Minato ward's "Central Park" in terms of the recreational opportunities and the connection to nature that it provides in the midst of metropolis. The Prince Arisugawa Memorial Park's grounds also house

Prince Arisugawa.

the Tokyo Metropolitan Library, the library Ami likely visits regularly.

The park was named after a Prince who lived in the mid-nineteenth century, and the famous statue of him that we see in the park dates from 1903. The statue was not originally in this location; it was near the Diet building (the Japanese parliament building) and moved to this park later, when it was dedicated to the Prince. The statue now faces the Tokyo Metropolitan Library.[11]

This park was seen quite often in the series, as it provided a 'forested' environment in the middle of the big city. When the animators wanted a nature backdrop as opposed to the standard cityscape backgrounds of the series, they often brought the characters to this park. Furthermore, the characters are quite enthusiastic about this particular park. Ami comes when she does not have her cram school sessions because, according to her, "It's very peaceful." Flower enthusiast Makoto Kino lives near the park, matching her green personality.

Mitsui Club
Mita

In a famous episode of the anime, Usagi fails a "Princess Seminar" held in Madame Rose's Mansion. That mansion is modeled on the mansion now known as the Mitsui Club and the design is similar to the building called the *Rokumeikan*.

The Rokumeikan, or "Deer Cry Pavilion," represented the culmination of the early Meiji government's ideology of architectural representation (late 19th century). With increasing numbers of foreign dignitaries visiting Japan at the time, the Meiji government needed to provide adequate accommodation for them. Initially the government used the *Enryokan* situated within the Hama Detached Palace in Tokyo, but this building was refurbished only as a stopgap solution. Eventually, they had to build a custom-designed building.

In 1880, with the support of Kaoru Inoue, the powerful minister of foreign affairs, a 100,000 yen budget for the Rokumeikan was approved and the commission for its design awarded to Josiah Conder (1852-1920), an architect trained in London. In 1912, it was turned into a place for western-style social activities, and, in 1992, Madame Rose used this similar-looking mansion to unleash the horror of Minako and Rei's dancing upon the unsuspecting feet of hired help.

Keiō Private University

The school that Mamoru Chiba (Tuxedo Mask) and his friend Motoki attend in the manga, KO University, is based on Keiō University, the oldest private university in Japan. Many of the older *Sailor Moon* characters are students at the school. In the manga both Motoki and his girlfriend Reika attend Keiō. Also a student here is Sailor Pluto, Setsuna Meiō, a major in theoretical physics.

Keiō is the most elite of Japan's private universities. Consider it Japan's Harvard or Yale. Even those who can pass its rigorous entrance examination need a lot of money to attend. Many of the characters who go to Keiō are very smart and could easily have attended the public Tokyo University—a cheaper school—instead. Takeuchi chose Keiō, however, as a reflection of her own background in Minato ward. She was a student here, and wanted to ground her series in the Tokyo she knew.

Akasaka Hikawa Shrine
Akasaka

The Azabu Hikawa Shrine is the Hikawa shrine depicted in the *Sailor Moon* manga, but the animators of the anime series modeled their Hikawa Shrine on the Akasaka Hikawa Shrine (also in Minato ward). The main difference between the Akasaka and Azabu Hikawa Shrines visually are a set of ascending stairs and layout. The real Akasaka Shrine and the anime Azabu Shrine are identical on both counts.

The shrine at Akasaka has a unique history all its own. Established sometime between 641 and 974 CE, the original shrine was not a Hikawa shrine, having been built before the denomination existed. Previously, the shrine was located one kilometer north, where Akasaka Middle School now stands. In 1730 it was moved by the 8th Tokugawa Shogun, Yoshimune, and became his personal shrine.[12]

Why did the animators use this shrine rather than

the one used in the manga? Maybe because the site provides striking views of Tokyo for the anime series. From the beautiful spring scene featured as the girls walk up the steps during the *Ami's First Love* special, to the eerie sunset as the shadow of ultimate evil, Galaxia, looms over Tokyo in the last season, the Akasaka Shrine gave poetic license that would be unimaginable with the Azabu Shrine, and became a hallmark of the series.

Bridal Shop
Minami Aoyama

In the manga's fifth act, as Usagi and Makoto pass a famous bridal boutique, they see a mannequin of a bride in the store's window, overlooking the street. Passers-by note the bridal dress has a curse on it; whomever buys the dress will carry a ghost with her, causing great misfortune. When Usagi and Makoto overhear this conversation, a chilling voice calls out, "I am the ghost of the bride!"

This shop is based on an actual store in the Aoyama area, which did in fact have a mannequin wearing a bridal gown looking over the street at the time the series ran. Naoko Takeuchi was apparently a fan of a television program in which two characters would constantly bicker in front of the store's façade.

The inclusion of such detail shows the extent to which the manga reflected the Tokyo that its author, Naoko Takeuchi, was familiar with. But the animators who created the cartoon series were familiar with a different part of Tokyo, Roppongi, which came to be reflected in their interpretation of the series.

Roppongi

Located next to Azabu-Jûban is Jûban's naughty sibling, Roppongi. Ask a Westerner who's been to Tokyo what he remembers of Roppongi, and you might find his memory a tad hazy. Filled with bright lights, cold drinks, and a lot of love hotels, Roppongi sleeps by day and lives by night. But Roppongi's transformation into a red light district did not occur until the 1970s, when discos and bars started moving to the area in droves, catering to the large foreign population which had begun living in the area.

While even most Japanese see Roppongi as a rather drab district culturally, like much of Tokyo, it has significant history. Waley notes that Roppongi literally means "Six Trees," and while those six trees no longer exist, the name remains. The names of the six trees were actually allusions; there were once six feudal lords who ran the area, and each portion of Roppongi was named after a different tree whose characteristic the lord shared.

Trees are very important to local Roppongi mythology for other reasons. One of the great apostles of Japanese Buddhism, Shinran, visited the temple Zenpukuji in Roppongi (then a part of Azabu-Jûban) in the thirteenth century. Before leaving the temple, he planted his staff upside down and into the ground, saying that if his teachings would find favor with the people, his staff would grow into a great tree. And indeed, the Ginko tree sitting on the grounds of the temple is over 750 years old. It had long been designated a natural monument until it was severely burned in the air raids of 1945 and thought dead, its designation lifted. The tree later burst back to life and was made a natural monument again. Perhaps this was partly the inspiration for the *Makaijû* arc (involving a demonic tree) of the second anime season, a storyline unique to the anime.[13]

Roppongi Tunnel & Asahi Television

There are more Roppongi connections to the Makaijû storyline. Like their depiction of the Rainbow Bridge, the writers of the *Sailor Moon* anime made use of a new structure that was finished around the time the second season began to air: they had an enemy attack the sailor soldiers in a newly-opened tunnel. The Roppongi tunnel was finished and opened for traffic around 1993, and became a battlefield in an episode that aired almost immediately afterward.

Another Roppongi site became a battlefield in the second episode of the Makaijû storyline. The plot revolved

around the girls being invited to screen test for a part in an upcoming drama to be filmed by an "Ashita Television Studios."

An "Asahi Television Station" is located in the same area where Ashita would be if it were real.

Asahi Television also happens to be the same station that broadcast the *Sailor Moon* anime series, and its buildings are exactly as depicted in the series. Just as Takeuchi used the Azabu-Jûban she knew in creating her series, the animation studio's writers reflected their home—Roppongi—in their anime episodes.

A short distance from here is the place where the Asahi TV station got its name from: the Asahi Shinto Shrine, established around the same time as Azabu's Hikawa Shrine. The shrine received its name from a Priestess-Princess named Asahi who spent much of her life there, although the name was not changed to Asahi until the turn of the twentieth century.

Tōyo Eiwa Girls Academy

Shrine maiden Rei Hino (Sailor Mars) attends a school called "T*A Private Girls Academy," a Catholic religious school. Her school is based on a well known school called "Tōyo Eiwa Girls Academy," located near Azabu-Jûban. The real Azabu Hikawa shrine that is the model for manga Rei's Hikawa shrine is within walking distance of the school.

Tōyo Eiwa is a Methodist missionary school, founded in 1884 and includes an "elevator" middle and high school where the students do not have to take a test to get into the high school. It is known in Japan as a training school for elite girls. Near the middle and high school grounds, there are also kindergarten and grade school sections. American architect William M. Boris designed the plans for the main buildings in 1884. The school buildings were erected starting in the late nineteenth century, and a great  deal of Western architecture was brought to Japan because of these schools.

For a deeper history of the school, we must travel back a decade before its founding. In 1873, the Wesleyan Methodist Church of Canada selected two missionaries to be sent to Japan for the first time. In 1881, the Methodist Church in Canada established a woman's missionary society and decided to send one of its members to Japan. The school claims this was partly based on requests from missionaries in Japan who said there was a need for missionary women.

Martha J. Cartmell arrived in Japan at the end of 1882. She set about promulgating Christianity, being especially enthusiastic about organizing Bible classes for women. She decided there was a need to establish a girls high school. At about the same time, the Mission headquarters in Canada started to contemplate the possibility of establishing a boarding school in Tokyo.

The purchase of a piece of land in Azabu made it possible for the school to be started, with two students, in October 1884. November 6 was designated as the official date for the opening of the school. Reflecting a time of great Western influence on Japan, there was remarkable increase in the number of students enrolled as the years passed.

With an additional new building, a primary school was added in 1888, and in 1889 what was later to become a senior high school was established. However, advancing deterioration of the main building forced the original school buildings to be demolished in August of 1993 (they stood for over a century— an impressive feat for Japanese architecture) and new buildings were erected. In *Sailor Moon,* the T*A logo is the same as Tōyo Eiwa's before the buildings were demolished.[14]

Why does Rei, a Shinto shrine priestess, attend a Christian religious school? Rei's father is a prominent politician; he likely wanted her to go to a school for the elite, which the T*A Private Girls academy seems to be.

A brief detour into the Sailor V manga

The *Sailor V* manga, the prequel to *Sailor Moon*, is also set in Minato ward. In the first four seasons of the anime, Sailor Venus's alter-ego Minako Aino even goes to a different middle school from the other girls, in Shiba Koen, denoting a connection to her former "Sailor V" persona (when most of the activity occurred in that area rather than Azabu-Jûban).

Meiji Shrine Outer Gardens – "Ginko Tree Row"
Yoyogi

In a memorable scene from *Sailor V*, Minako Aino kisses her crush on a tree-lined street. This street, called Ginko Tree Row, is located on the property of the Meiji Shrine, which owns a huge tract of expensive land in the heart of of Tokyo. The beautiful but secluded Inner Garden is 72 hectares, and the vast Outer Garden (where the public can roam) is not just a garden but practically a city within the city. In addition to the Meiji Memorial Gallery and the main Hall (now almost exclusively a wedding chapel), there are various sports stadiums.

When the Olympics came to Tokyo in 1964, the Olympic Committee built all the athletes' lodgings and stadiums here; when the Olympics were over, they tore down the lodgings but kept the stadiums. (Broadcasting company NHK also moved into the grounds once the lodgings were gone.) The sports-loving Takeuchi integrated the open, green fields and stadiums that the Outer Gardens offer into the manga featuring her sports-loving sailor heroine, Sailor V.

Shiba Koen

While most of the sailor soldiers live in Azabu, the bouncy Minako Aino lives in Shiba Koen, another district in Minato ward. The districts of Minato have very different personalities from each other (the fiery Rei of the anime lives very close to Roppongi and has a 'Roppongi feel' to her), and there is a big difference between Shiba Koen and the other Minato neighborhoods. Maybe that is what makes Minako stand out?

Tokyo historian Paul Waley calls Shiba (meaning "lawn") a place that has been "twice transformed." In the Edo period (1603-1868) it was a city of Buddhist temples. At the start of Japan's Meiji period (1868-1912), it underwent its first transformation. The Meiji leaders wanted to use Shintoism, as opposed to Buddhism, as a way to unite the Japanese people under a common religion, and to distinguish themselves from the previous rulers of Japan, the Shoguns. Buddhism was a symbol of both something alien to Japan (having come from China) and the Shogunate which had practiced and promoted it.

As a result, Buddhism was repressed and the wealth of Buddhist temples confiscated. Shiba Koen's Zojoji, the personal temple of the Tokugawas (the Shogun leaders from 1603-1868), was the wealthiest, strongest, and hardest hit. The Meiji government expropriated the lands and turned them into a park, one of Tokyo's first. The word "koen" means park, so Shiba became *Shiba Koen*—the Lawn Park.

Shiba's second transformation turned it into what you see today—the air raids of World War II destroyed much of Shiba's temples, and in their place Shiba Koen grew luxury hotels, golf clubs… and a giant tower. (More on that in a bit.) Shiba is somewhat of an oddity. On the outside, one sees glitz, glamour, and excitement, but behind the glitz, Shiba is calm, serene, and contemplative. It sounds a bit like Minako.[15]

Minato Public Onarimon Elementary School
Shiba Koen

Minako Aino spent her junior high school days at Onarimon Middle School. If the series took place today, though, she could not be a student there. While it was a middle school when the series ran, it is now an elementary school.

The school has many connections to Takeuchi's works. The main character from another of her manga series, *The Cherry Project*'s Chieri Asuka, was an alumna of the junior high school here. And Usagi's teacher, Haruna Sakurada, worked here as Chieri's instructor as well.

Worthy of note about Shiba Koen is the importance of gates to the modern naming conventions. Shiba, until the construction of the Tokyo Tower, was mainly known as the location of the Zojoji temple, the place where the Tokugawa Shoguns were honored. At one point, it spanned hundreds of buildings, but today only a few of the buildings' gates are left.

Temple gates are small structures protected by deities; you would have to pass through these in order to get to the main parts of Zojoji. One was called Onarimon, the gate once taken by the Shoguns themselves when they came to visit the temple, and the structure from which this school received its name. Another notable gate is *Sakuradamon* or the "Cherry Blossom gate." One of the main thoroughfares of Minato ward, Sakurada Avenue, is named after it, and Usagi's teacher Haruna Sakurada was probably named after it in turn.[16]

Tokyo Jikei-e Medical Sciences School
Nishi Shinbanshi

Sailor Mercury's alter-ego, the young genius Ami Mizuno,

dreams of attending Tokyo Jikei-e Medical School, referred to as "J Medical School" in the series. It is one of the top medical schools in Japan, and her family already has a history there.

The hospital's name stands for "Mercy and Love" and was the first Japanese school whose specialization was the medical sciences. In addition to the medical science school, there is a general hospital which is supposedly the best hospital in Tokyo, if not all of Japan. Ami's mother graduated from that same school of medicine, and works at that hospital.

Kyoritsu College of Pharmacy

How does Takeuchi know Shiba so well? Why is she so fascinated with Minato ward and Tokyo's bay area? Why do all her works feature these locations? There is a single answer to these questions: this is where she lived, worked, and drew her manga. Takeuchi is an alumna of this college of pharmacy located in Shiba Koen, and debuted her first manga serial, *Love Call*, while she was a student here.

After earning her degree, Takeuchi worked at Keiō Hospital as a licensed pharmacist but eventually gave up her interest in medicine (could Ami's dreams of being a doctor have any relation to hers?) to follow her passion for writing manga.[17]

Tokyo Tower

Those who became fans of the *Sailor Moon* series by watching the English dub on television when they were children often thought the series took place in France, and with good reason. Was that not the Eiffel Tower in the background?

Frequently seen in the show, the tall structure is not the Eiffel Tower but rather the Tokyo Tower. Standing 333 meters tall (including the antennae), some consider it to be the symbol of Tokyo. In the *Sailor Moon* manga and anime it served that role, but became a battleground several times as well.

The observatory deck was completed in 1967, to the delight of lazy teachers who often use it as a field trip spot. Originally, the deck was just a maintenance platform, but now it provides visitors with a spectacular view of Tokyo, particularly at night. The tower itself is lit up by 164 lights, which illuminate the rising figure.

Even those who consider such tourist sites an eyesore tend to admit after seeing it lit up at night that the Tower

is something spectacular, glittering above all the other high rises in the city.

Furthermore, the tower provides a vital service. The tower broadcasts eight television frequencies, four FM radio frequencies, and numerous public service stations. All in all there are nearly 70 TV and radio channels being beamed out from the tower to homes in the eastern part of Honshu. (The main Japanese island.) One station, Tokyo Television, actually has its studio at the bottom of the tower.

The tower was constructed in Shiba because of its advantageous location for broadcast to eastern Japan. And in fact, Shiba has more connections to electricity. Electronics makers NEC, Toshiba (aka "Tokyo Shibaura Denki"—*denki* means electricity) and Oki Denki all have their headquarters in Shibaura, on the southern edge of Shiba Koen.

Heading toward infinity
Tennōzu Isle

The island on which much of the third arc of the *Sailor Moon* manga (third season of the anime) takes place is called *Mugensu* Island; meaning Infinity Island. In our world it is called *Tennōzu Isle,* a man-made island inside Tokyo Bay that has become known for being futuristic and high-tech. All the buildings there were created using modern architectural techniques, in a style that highlights sharp angles and attracts the eye.

Tennōzu Isle is fairly easy to get to from Minato ward. The Tokyo Monorail from Hamamatsucho station can get to Tennōzu Isle in around five minutes.[18]

Tennōzu Sphere Tower
Shinagawa ward—Higashi Shinagawa

Professor Sōichi Tomoe, the evil mastermind of *Sailor Moon*'s third arc, is the owner of the *Mugen* (Infinity) Academy building. His tall structure overlooks Tokyo Bay, on the newest, most fashionable island in the area.

The actual Mugen Academy building is called the

Tennōzu Sphere Tower and opened in 1993, shortly before the third arc of the *Sailor Moon* manga began being serialized. The two buildings look *exactly* alike.

At a height of 120 meters, the Sphere Tower is 27 stories tall, but it is not a school. The real Mugen Academy is an office space tower, and is used by companies and independent organizations; it's especially become popular among the IT crowd.

What would Sphere Tower be without a similarly named convention center? Tennōzu Sphere Tower has two: the Art Sphere and the Sphere MEX. Michiru Kaiō, the elegant alter-ego of Sailor Neptune, held concerts at the Art Sphere.

Sea Fort Square Hall

While the outside of the Sphere Tower mirrors the Mugen Academy building, the inside is very different. Its first floor actually resembles that of another building located next to the Art Sphere, called Sea Fort Square. Across the street from Sea Fort Square is the Tennōzu monorail station which the girls take to get there.

The trio of buildings that surround the Mugen Academy building in the manga are called the "Towers" in our world, and yet another building, the North Pier Takeshiba building near Hamamatsucho, is the what the manga's buildings are modeled after. The Central Tower is located behind the Sphere Tower in reality, but the North Pier Takeshiba is not.

Ebara Shinto Shrine
Kita-Shinagawa

There is a fascinating connection between Tennōzu and the three Talismans sought by Sailors Uranus, Neptune, and Pluto in the third arc. Perhaps Takeuchi knew this when she chose the island for her story.

    The enshrined deity of the nearby Ebara Shinto shrine is named Gozu Tennō; this is another name for Lord Susanō, who first obtained the three treasures (Talismans). Each year this shrine has a "Southern Tennō" festival in his honor. The island received its name in connection with this temple's deity, the original wielder of the Talismans.[19]

Tokyo Travels

Not all the action in *Sailor Moon* takes place in Minato ward; some takes place in other areas of Tokyo as well. Here are a few features and places connected to the city that are located within the city's vicinity.

Tokyo's Drainage Ditches & Waterways

A previously unknown junior member of the Taira clan took the name of *Edo*, Mouth of the River, after the location of his house. He settled in Chichibu to build himself a house in the latter part of the twelfth century, and he did so near the river's end, thus gaining what was soon to be a famous name. Many centuries later, Tokyo's founder Ōta Dōkan built a castle there, the "Castle at Edo," and bequeathed the Edo name upon the town that would eventually grow into the city of Tokyo.

Tokyo's history is inseparable from its environment and the natural disasters that have befallen it. Two distinct but contrasting events occurred constantly: fire and flooding. Until brick and cement became the standard in the twentieth century, fire could not be avoided. Tokyo's citizens found it surprising when there was not a massive fire within a two-year span (and almost considered it an omen), so they developed their buildings with a less permanent mold in mind.[20]

Flooding was tamed by damming and draining the many rivers that flowed throughout Tokyo. The rivers that crossed Tokyo are still identified with the city, but many in the older sections of Tokyo, like Minato ward, had long been cemented over by the time the sailors soldiers came around. Seen in many anime, and very often in *Sailor Moon*, are various—and massive—cement flood-drainage ditches. Some are canals that buildings are built into, while others are strictly for drainage purposes; both are featured as battlefields in various *Sailor Moon* anime episodes.

Although the rivers are tamed, flooding remains a concern in the bay area of Tokyo; after all, it is located on the waterfront. Thus the ditches remain. Famed Tokyo scholar Maeda Ai once lamented the expansion of the cement ditches which had paved over the rivers that Edo was known for, but noted that those rivers still run, hidden under the pavement; much like Edo itself.[21]

Jindai Botanical Park
Chofû City

Featured in the beautiful opening of *Sailor Moon*'s first feature film was an expansive botanical garden, which is located a short distance from Minato, in Chofû city. It was founded in 1957 by the Tokyo Metropolitan Government and is named after a nearby temple. Home to over 100,000 plants from 3,000 species, it is the most complete botanical park in Tokyo.

Two flowers play prominent roles in the opening sequence wherein the sailor soldiers visit the *Jindai* ("Age of the Gods") Botanical Park. The first is the rose, the emblem flower of Mamoru (Tuxedo Mask) who is Usagi's boyfriend and accompanies her to the park. Roses from around the world are found blooming here all year long, just as they were depicted in the film. The second flower featured in the movie was a "Forget-Me-Not," which our protagonist pointed out to Mamoru, and in this the film was incorrect. The park lacks "Forget-Me-Not" flowers.

Toei Animation Studio
Nerima ward, Tokyo

Referred to as *Ginga* (Galaxy) Television in the fifth season of the anime, Toei studios was the portal to the villain Galaxia's lair, where the sailor soldiers' final battle took place. The Toei animation studio has a rich 50-year history,

among whose crown jewels has been the *Pretty Soldier Sailor Moon* anime series. In addition to being Japan's biggest animation production company, Toei Animation Co. also boasts the longest history of any company in the Japanese animation industry, having been established in 1956 by Toei after it merged with Nichido Film. The company has produced a large number of hit animation films and series including *Galaxy Express 999*, *Dragon Ball,* and, of course, *Sailor Moon.*

Although the company had many successes in Japan, Asia, and Europe, it was relatively unknown in the United States until September 1995, when *Dragon Ball* and *Sailor Moon* were screened one after another in syndication. *Sailor Moon* also began broadcast in Germany, Sweden, and Greece that October. It became massively popular in all those countries and recorded many merchandise sales records.

Yokohama Foreign Cemetery & Chinatown
Yokohama, Japan

Yokohama is a huge port city near Tokyo. With a population of over three million people, it is Japan's second-largest city. One of Yokohama's features is its concentration of foreigners and foreign culture. This is a result of treaties following the Meiji revolution that changed Japan in the late nineteenth century. As we mentioned with Azabu, foreigners tended to concentrate in specific areas (mainly, those areas where they were *allowed* to live and work). Yokohama was one of those places.

When Usagi's friend Naru is mourning the loss of her lover Nephrite in the first *Sailor Moon* season, she heads to Yokohama to find solace. Yokohama has one of the only

cemeteries in Japan. While there are many churches in Tokyo, none have cemeteries. Japanese law states that native citizens must be cremated rather than buried. Thus, few western-style cemeteries have been built, and nearly all of them are for foreign residents. The Yokohama Foreign Cemetery, furthermore, is mainly for foreigners who made specific contributions to Japanese society. Naru saw Yokohama's cemetery as a holy place where foreigners like Nephrite would be laid to rest, so that is where she went.

At the cemetery, Usagi and Naru's friend, Umino, says he is hungry for Peking Duck. Perhaps the smells from nearby Yokohama Chinatown were wafting toward the graveyard. Yokohama's Chinatown is the largest of its kind in the country. A huge, vermilion Chinese gate greets visitors at each of the four entrances, and one large gate in the middle marks the entrance to the main road. We even see Makoto pass through a gate on her way to meet Usagi at the cemetery. Each gate is a different color, representing a different season and element, and is dedicated to a different god for protection of the area. For example, the west gate has bright colors painted onto its white base and brings peace to the neighborhood according to legend. Yokohama Chinatown also abounds with restaurants and specialty shops selling goods not available anywhere else in the country. Over 500 shops and eateries pack the Chinatown, as do many visitors who come to sample the fare.

As long as we are on the subject of food...

The Azabu Food/Culture Tour

The locations in this section do not appear in the series, but most are connected to it in some way. If you are visiting Minato ward and want to get the full *Sailor Moon* experience, taking in these sights, sounds, and tastes, is highly recommended.

Tanuki Hill

A *tanuki* is a "raccoon-dog"; it is not a raccoon (although it looks like one) and it belongs to the canine family. In Japanese lore they are said to be magical and have shape-shifting powers

A park in the Tanuki Hill area.

that they use for either benevolent or malevolent purposes depending on their personality. In Japanese legends, the tanuki—although it can change into anything— often assumes the form of a monk to play tricks on people.

They are said to love *sake* (Japanese rice-wine): statues and pictures of them often depict the Tanuki with a sake bottle in one hand and a promissory note to pay for it in the other. In Japanese mythology, tanuki get blurred with stories of *kitsune* (foxes) who are said to be the messengers of the Shinto god *Inari*. Foxes also have transformation powers and play tricks on people. Due to a number of legends about raccoon transformations in Azabu, many places are named after tanuki. For instance, Tanukizaka (Tanuki Slope) in Moto-Azabu and

Mamianazaka (Mamiana Slope) in Azabu are written with the characters for tanuki.

It is said that people who pass by these places are often 'enchanted.' Due to the belief of magical animals and transformations in the district, it is easy to imagine people in Azabu-Jûban chalking up the appearance of mysterious sailor soldiers and related incidents to tanuki sightings or tanuki-induced illusions.[22]

Additionally, the flower shop run by the witch Tellu in the third season of *Sailor Moon,* "Flower Shop Mamiana," is based on a flower shop that really exists on Mamiana street. Mamiana Street received its name because the third Tokugawa shogun, Iemitsu, supposedly spotted a tanuki on the street while on his way to the shogunal medicine gardens.

Jûban Inari Shrine

The Jûban Inari shrine is a small Shinto shrine that was located in Azabu-Jûban long before the area received its current name (although it has only been in its present location more recently). Inari is a fox deity and god of harvests, and in Japanese mythology foxes are considered magical—and  sometimes dangerous—animals. There are many stories of foxes pulling pranks and foxes turning into humans.

In modern Japan, Inari shrines are often connected to business. Those who run businesses go to one often to see guidance, as the fox is supposed to bring good luck; for example, Theodore Bestor wrote in his recent ethnography, *Tsukiji,* that many sellers at the Tsukiji fish market often drop a few coins into the Inari shrine across the street before they start their day.[23]

Five posts depicting five gods enshrined as deities are located at the shrine. They are supposedly the five guardian gods of Jûban town. This is similar to the five sailor soldiers (Moon, Mercury, Mars, Jupiter, and Venus) who watch over the area in *Sailor Moon.*

Azabu-Jûban Hot Springs / Koshi Hot Baths

Onsen, or hot springs, are a very popular form of recreation in Japan. Many baths are located across the country, their springs staying warm even in the snow. In one episode of *Sailor Moon,* Usagi's family takes a trip to an onsen (likely in northern Japan). This was a mixed-sex resort, which probably means they went to one of the older ones.

In Japan, vending machines are everywhere, even by the front doors of onsen.

The hot springs are popular today, but some onsen, and even public bathhouses, refuse foreigners. There is a famous case of a foreigner who managed to gain Japanese citizenship (quite a feat, in fact) but was still refused admittance into his town's baths. They are one of Japan's true cultural wonders, but this case bring to light Japan's historical legacy of racism.

There are also hot springs located in Usagi's Azabu-Jûban district, one of which is called the "Koshi hot baths." It is one of the only in the area fed by a natural spring.

Cool of the Evening Festival
Azabu-Jûban

In August 1995, an episode of *Sailor Moon*'s fourth season aired which featured a foreign princess lost in a *matsuri* (festival) taking place in Azabu-Jûban. Not coincidentally, the date this episode aired was the perfect time to take in the Azabu-Jûban "Cool of the Evening" festival which occurs in late August every year, and lasts for three days.

It is the biggest festival the Jûban shopping district has, and due to Jûban's own uniqueness, is unlike many other festivals held around Tokyo. Around the Ichinohashi park (featured frequently in the anime series and seen in the R movie) all the various embassies gather round and have their own food booths. You are able to try the many delicacies of the world in one location! And as seen in the picture, it is just as crowded as it was in the series.

Watanabe no Tsuna

There is a slope in the Mita neighborhood of Minato ward named after a man called Watanabe no Tsuna. In fact, the whole area has come to be named after him. A building manager in the second act of the manga also happens to be called Watanabe no Tsuna. Where does this name come from and why is it so popular?[24]

Watanabe no Tsuna was one of the first *Shitennō*; the

word which is used to refer to the four Dark Kingdom generals of the first manga arc. Shitennō means "Four Heavenly Kings" and comes from Buddhist mythology, which sees the four portions of the sky: north, south, east, and west, each ruled by a separate lord.

The *Heike Monogatari* is a famous book of Japanese mythology where the term Four Heavenly Kings was used for the first times in Japanese history. The phrase referred to the retainers of Minamoto no Yorimitsu (948-1021), one of the most powerful Japanese generals.

A slope in the Watanabe no Tsuna area.

Unlike the *Sailor Moon* villains who have stolen the Four Heavenly Kings' name, the original four—as well as Yorimitsu—were famed demon slayers in Japanese lore. They vanquished ogres, highway robbers, and even giant spiders. All became famous individually, with Sakata no Kintoki (also known as Kintaro) rising to the highest prominence. He grew up with wild animals (it is said that a bear could not beat him in sumo wrestling), always carried a hatchet, and could push down trees by himself. But Tsuna too was well known; the title of Akira Kurosawa's famous film Rashomon is based on Watanabe no Tsuna's legendary slaying of a demon at Rasho gate (aka the "Rasho mon"). Watanabe no Tsuna is also the warrior who protects the Azabu Hikawa shrine's gate.

Although *Sailor Moon* could appear to a foreign audience to take place in any city, as we have seen, it distinctly reflects the capital of Japan, Tokyo. Yet *Sailor Moon* is a reflection of the Japanese society in which it is situated as well, and it is there that we now turn.

Family

*F*amily, or *kazoku* in Japanese, has been a key force in all forms of livelihood in Japan for centuries; until modern times, all generations of a family lived under one roof, from grandparents to grandchildren. What we see in *Sailor Moon*, therefore, is a distinctly modern notion of family, one centered on parents' relationship to their children, and not the traditional concept of kazoku as a clan. But the depiction of family in *Sailor Moon* is not a simple one, indeed *Sailor Moon* goes to great lengths to show the complexities of family life in Japan.

Through its diverse cast of characters, *Sailor Moon* has managed to present to audiences varying pictures of Japanese families. From the relatively stable family units of Usagi Tsukino and Minako Aino to the single parent (or guardian, as the case may be) families of Ami Mizuno and Rei Hino (one the product of divorce, and the other of abandonment) down to the orphaned lives of Makoto Kino and Mamoru Chiba, the series reflects the great diversity of family life in modern Japan. For some of them, family life can be cold and lonely, but all characters manage to persevere, no matter their handicap.

The Japanese family system as we know it today is a product of the home revolution of the early twentieth century. Wanting to promote Western practices of living, enthusiasts of progress called upon other Japanese to adopt a western system focused around the wife and child. For example, until "everyday life reform" (as it was called), families would not eat around a table together; instead, they all had separate trays and ate according to their generational rank. Wives and mothers were not considered the cooks of their households, either. Often, they had a maid or a daughter-in-law to prepare meals for them while they supervised. Only around 1910 were there calls for "home reform" to make the position of wife a job. And it was starting then that the close and central family we see in the Tsukino household of *Sailor Moon* actually came to be the ideal.[25]

The Tsukino Family Tree

Family matters—particularly when it comes to the way the sailor soldiers have grown up. Each girl's life is indelibly connected to her family history, and we see this in the girls' various personalities. Ami, for example, inherited her drive to be a doctor from her mother. Rei's strong-willed personality comes from her politician father. (In the manga, this is also correlated to her quiet nature; she is still upset at him for never being there when she was growing up, especially when her mother died.) Makoto is tough because she has had to fend for herself most of her life, having lost her parents at a young age. Minako and Usagi are the only two who have both parents, and Usagi has a sibling to boot, which the series implies is part of the reason for their buoyant personalities.

Indeed, Usagi's parents, Kenji and Ikuko, are both outgoing and involved in their daughter's life (making sure she gets good grades, looking out for what boys she's dating, etc.) This is certainly part of what makes Usagi the cheerful, outgoing girl that she is; few of her friends can say their families are the same, and all of them rely on Usagi as their guiding light.

Usagi is fourteen when the series starts, and her parents are implied to have married in their early 20s. The age of her parents is relevant because marrying age has become a major issue in the Japanese media since *Sailor Moon* began its original run. Surveys have shown that Japanese women are waiting longer and longer before getting married. Many

Japanese used to think that a woman over 30 had missed her chance to marry. But now, sometimes women wait until their late 20s or later, if they get married at all. A phenomenon called the *make inu* or "lost dog" has become well-known, where women may refuse to get married at all rather than be tied to a household.

IKUKO TSUKINO — KENJI TSUKINO

↓

USAGI TSUKINO   SHINGO TSUKINO

Usagi's mother is a homemaker in every incarnation of the series, and her father Kenji is usually a newspaper editor It is implied from what the family owns that he makes a lot of money. The house they live in is two stories and very large for Jûban, they also own car in Tokyo and go on several vacations. They are a very stable, well-off family.

The anime and manga Kenji was often shown having enough free time to be involved in his children's lives. In the live action *Sailor Moon* series that aired in 2003, the writers of the series rewrote the Kenji character to cover a problem in contemporary Japanese life (that was less popularly discussed at the time *Sailor Moon* had originally aired): the missing father.

A child in Japan may not see his or her father for weeks or months at a time—even if he is living at home—because the father's work occupies so much of his time and takes him to another city. Some of these fathers and husbands will try to remain at home but face 2-3 hour (or longer) commutes to their offices. They often get home long past the child's bedtime and are off to the morning train well before their kids wake up to go to school. In this manner, a lot of kids could sympathize with the plight of the revised Tsukino family.

Lifting the Genius Veil
An investigation into Ami's family life

Where did Usagi's friend, the genius Ami Mizuno (Sailor Mercury), get her mental prowess from? Could she have inherited it from her parents, a doctor and an artist—people whom are likely geniuses as well? Sigmund Freud, the famed psychologist, suggested that children's intelligence results partially from their genetics, and partly from their childhood environment.

Ami's hobbies are swimming, chess, reading, and studying. Swimming and chess are supposed to be quite effective in training your brain, and of course, Ami reads at the beach, on the train—*everywhere.*

But another source of Ami's genius is clearly her mother. Ami's mother has had an immense impact on her life, and not just in passing on her genes. In a December 1992 issue of the Japanese anime magazine *Animage,* there was an illustration by Takeuchi called "Medical Student Ami." According to the caption on the illustration, Ami's mother is a graduate of "J Medical School" in Azabu-Jûban, based on the famous Tokyo Jikei-e Medical Science University near Shiba Koen.

The Animage article states that Ami's aim had always been to go to the university her mother attended, and that she did indeed make it in. Notable in the illustration is that Ami wants to be "on the frontier of new research, just like [her] mother."[26]

Yet Ami's mother is only half the story. Ami's father must be investigated to fully understand her success.

While her father never appears in any series, we see hints of him in both the anime and the manga. And, in one anime magazine, Ami's family registry was printed. The family registry is one of the most important records kept by the local government in Japan. The family registry is changed on any occasion that deal with the issue of family in Japan: for example, when people marry, have children, and get divorced. In a divorce, children who are listed under their father will keep their father's name, and most do get listed with the father just for this reason. Not surprisingly, Ami is listed with her father as the parent.

While we know for sure Ami's parents are divorced, for a while people were unsure as to whether he simply moved out or if he died. Ami put the question to rest in the May 1993 issue of Nakayoshi. Her father is still living and he is a painter. In fact, he sends her a painting in the fourth season of the anime.

The series states that Usagi was Ami's first friend (of her own age.) Ami's father was likely her best friend for most of her younger life, so the divorce must have shaken her hard. We know that they had a fairly close relationship because we are told in an issue of Nakayoshi that Ami's father was a member of the same sports club that Ami attends, and that it was *he* who taught her how to swim and play chess. Ami owes much of her genius to her father's influence.[27]

Due to the vastly irregular time schedules between the two parents (one a doctor, the other a painter), it is likely that they never saw each other. While this is common among married people in modern Japan, they usually do not get divorced. We are never told why the couple split, although an early anime episode hints at Ami's father as potentially having been abusive.

Also notable in terms of family life reflections is Ami's father's post-divorce treatment of his daughter. The only contact her father has with his daughter is sending her a sketch on her birthday (in the manga) and once in a while a painting (in the anime). That is pretty neglectful, but common in Japanese divorces, where the non-custodial parent typically drops out of sight.

Head and Shoulders Above the Rest

Few kids would want to end up in the same circumstances as tomboyish orphan Makoto Kino (Sailor Jupiter) when she began to live alone, but many would be envious of what could be called a teenager's dream: having an incredibly spacious apartment (by Tokyo standards) all to herself in a fabulous part of the city with all expenses paid and no adult supervision. But how does she get away with this?

Actually, it is not so unusual for a teenage girl in Tokyo to live by herself. Many teenagers to come to the city to study, or, in the case of the actresses who played the sailor soldiers in the live action *Sailor Moon* show, work. Tokyo is very expensive, and apartments there are very small, so it does not make economic sense for a family to move to there with their daughter. Other teenagers also live there by themselves because their parents are working overseas or do not come home until late at night, as is the case with Ami's mother.

Makoto's living alone can be seen from two different social commentary viewpoints. On one hand, Takeuchi is showing that a single girl can be strong and raise herself alone in Tokyo. This vibes with the "girl power" message of the series. Makoto Kino is the strongest of the sailor soldiers, and her ability to take care of herself shows that even though she is just a middle school girl, she is neither weak nor helpless.

On the other hand, Makoto is considered one of the loneliest characters in the series who—partially because of her broken home life—has lived an ostracized life. Although she is one of the tallest girls in her school, she is often teased by other girls in class for being a loner and violent, a problem the Japanese refer to as *ijime* or bullying. Had she been of average stature, the gossip that spread quickly her first day at Jûban Middle School probably would not have occurred, as the students would have no reason to be suspect of her.

The fact was, though, that Makoto was bigger than everyone else—so big that she could not even fit into their regular school uniforms—and that meant she was different from them. Standing out during one's school years is tough enough no matter where you live, but it is more difficult in a society like Japan where conformity is so important. Makoto shows us this in the first *Sailor Moon* movie, as she recalls what it was like to hear people talk about her:

> **Girl 1:** *"She injured someone again."*
> **Girl 2:** *"She'll be kicked out for sure this time."*
> **Girl 1:** *"Who cares? She's so violent."*

The audience knows that Makoto is a gentle person and would not intentionally injure someone (who was not harming someone else.) Makoto being violent is an assumption made by the others based upon her height. In *Sailor Moon* we see that bullying in Japan is something different from what we view as bullying in America. It is not the big kids preying upon the weak. It is the normal kids teasing those who stand out. Even though Makoto may be strong physically, she can be easily wounded by those weaker than her through verbal ijime.

This height ostracizing is not only a problem for her in school, but in romance as well. While her height makes her one of the strongest of the sailor soldiers, being a tall woman in Japanese society carries a severe stigma. As her crush "Crane Machine Joe" so eloquently put it, he doesn't like tall women, and Crane Machine Joe is not an exception. Like many men around the world, most Japanese men will not date women taller than them. For that matter, like their counterparts around the world, most Japanese women do not want men shorter than them, either.

At fourteen years old and around 5'6, Makoto is a full three inches taller than the average fully grown Japanese woman and an inch taller than the average Japanese man. We see ostracizing in her love life in the first episode in which she is introduced. She meets a man, "Crane Machine Joe," and practically stalks him, until he agrees to talk to her. When Makoto suggests that "it's happening all over again" after Crane Machine Joe rejects her for being "absurdly tall," it is probably because she is used to being rejected due to her height.

In a later *Sailor Moon* season episode this scenario occurs once more, reinforcing to the audience her ostracizing. She is ecstatic to attend a university dance party, believing that college-aged men would be tall enough to escort her. She develops a crush on one not just because he is handsome, but because he is willing to dance with someone so tall. The poor wallflower, when Ami asked why she was standing alone, had responded, "Ah, well, nobody would escort me, because I'm too tall..."

Culture and Lifestyle

S*ailor Moon* was considered a children's series when it ran as an anime on Japanese television. As a show aimed at kids, much of an episode's time was spent entertaining them. Yet the writers of the series often used it as an educational tool. The younger generation of Japan had become so inundated with Western culture that the anime often assumed an instructional role for promoting traditional Japanese culture to them. In the process, the series often served to parody Japanese culture as well, by having the characters fumble through traditions that were part of their culture but that they were unfamiliar with.

One episode of the third season serves as an example of how the anime both educates and parodies. In that episode, the protagonist, Usagi Tsukino (Sailor Moon) as well as her boyfriend Mamoru Chiba (Tuxedo Mask) and several friends, attend a "tea ceremony" with a young grand master (someone trained in the ceremony.) The traditional Japanese tea ceremony is characterized by the slow paced serving of fine green tea by the ceremony master, and stresses proper etiquette and patience, two ideals of Japanese culture. In the ceremony the person being served must sit on her knees as a sign of respect for the ritual.

When Usagi arrives, she must first be told how the tea ceremony works, thus educating a young audience which is likely unfamiliar with the ceremony. Then Usagi attempts to sit in the proper position during the ceremony. While Usagi's friends bear through the pain, the animators show that Usagi is hurting from having to sit in an uncomfortable position. Rather than bearing through it herself, however, she loses patience and ends up falling, almost causing an expensive teacup to break in the process.

Because the series did not assume knowledge of the Japanese tradition on the part of the viewer (shown in the need to explain the ceremony to Usagi), it was able to promote Japanese culture to non-Japanese viewers as well. Since the tea ceremony was explained, any non-Japanese viewer who was unfamiliar with it before watching gained knowledge of an ancient Japanese tradition. At the same time, it provided commentary on the lack of reverence for native tradition among some Japanese through parody.

Connected to culture is Japanese lifestyle. While the English definition of the word "lifestyle" is simply "a mode of living," the Japanese equivalent phrase, *seikatsu yōshiki*, means something much more vibrant. *Seikatsu* is everyday living: one's conditions, position, behavior, opinions, actions, and attitude toward life. It is a term with multiple connotations and great importance to the Japanese, and is used in a multitude of combinations, from *bunka seikatsu* (the "cultured life") to *gakusei seikatsu* (the "student life"). A person's varied seikatsu determines who they are, how they interact with others, and how others interact with them.

The main characters in *Sailor Moon* are characterized by their seikatsu. Minako's seikatsu is that of a free-wheeling student who loves video games; but she desires the seikatsu of a famous idol. Others, like Usagi's boyfriend, Mamoru, have the seikatsu of the wealthy, intelligent elite. In his public persona, he attends functions appropriate to the seikatsu he is living, like dinner parties with foreign dignitaries and culture festivals at his school. The seikatsu of cross-dressing Haruka Ten'ō (Sailor Uranus) is very different as well, and highlights the origins of her character as a result of Takeuchi's desire to have a character from the *takarazuka* theater tradition.

At first glance, the characters of *Sailor Moon* do not

behave in the mold of Western interpretations of Japanese lifestyle, with its insistence on formalities, politeness, and quiet. Usagi and the others are often impulsive, rude, and anything but the silent subway riders seen on PBS specials of Tokyo.

But they do not lead a Western seikatsu; the problem is that the Western interpretation of the Japanese lifestyle is far too simple. As it turns out, the characters of *Sailor Moon* are the products of the society they live in. From the Japanese education system that funnels students into tracks, to Japanese sensitivities about one's physical appearance, the layers of lifestyle depicted in *Sailor Moon* are highly complex, and closely reflect Japanese society as it really is.

The Deadly Poetics of the Sailor Soldiers

"Stop right there! Not only did you disturb a movie shoot, but you also chased after innocent people with a gun! You really are an outlaw! Wyatt Earp may, but we will never forgive you! In the name of the moon, we'll punish you!"

— Sailor Team to monster-of-the-week 'Western'

Among the many trademarks of *Sailor Moon* are the over-the-top introductory speeches the sailor soldiers make when confronting the "monster of the week." Containing everything from obscure cultural references to painful puns or even a series of verb conjugations, these speeches are as integral an accouterment to the sailor soldier as the sailor suits they wear.

But why bother to make these corny speeches at all? Why pose and posture before combat with a deadly enemy when the surer, more prudent course of action would be to simply charge in and attack? One response to this question might be "for the comedic value, of course,"—but what might surprise many is that there are myriad bases for these introductory speeches (albeit much more serious) in Japanese culture and literary tradition. The sailor soldiers' amusing introductory speeches are parodical amalgams of *jikoshōkai* (the formal self-introduction), *jisei* ("death poetry") and the behavior of warriors as exemplified in the thirteenth century Japanese literary masterwork, the *Heike Monogatari*.

Jikoshōkai

The *jikoshōkai,* or self-introduction, is a Japanese custom in which one introduces oneself to new people by giving a short autobiographical speech. Fans of anime in general may be familiar with this practice in the context of the classroom, where new students bow and present themselves to their classmates upon transferring into a new class.

Jikoshōkai is not restricted to classrooms, however, and is practiced in a variety of business and social contexts—indeed, in almost any situation where a person is entering a new group for the first time. An exchange between two characters during the fifth season of *Sailor Moon* illustrates the importance of jikoshōkai.

Aluminum Siren: *Thank you for the pizza! Pardon my late introduction... I'm Sailor Aluminum Siren! Nice to meet you!*

Lead Crow: *Uh? What's this greeting for?*

Aluminum Siren: *My mother told me that if I don't even say, "Hello," I can't be a respectable adult.*

In addition to *Sailor Moon*'s elaborate introductory speeches, jikoshōkai can also be fairly simple statements. For example, Usagi Tsukino's jikoshōkai to the audience (as seen in the first ten or so episodes of *Sailor Moon*) goes like this:

> *I'm Usagi Tsukino. Grade eight. I'm fourteen years old, a Cancer, with blood type O. My Birth stone is pearl. I guess I'm a bit clumsy and a crybaby. One day, I got a transformation brooch from a weird talking cat, Luna, and became a sailor soldier—and now she tells me I have to fight the bad guys. I'm not quite sure about that. Ah well. Things will work out somehow.*

Since, on one level, the sailor soldiers possess characteristics of typical Japanese school children that are parodies—for example, their warrior outfits lampoon the naval-style uniforms most schools have adopted for their students—it is tempting to say their introductory speeches are also parodies of jikoshōkai.

A parody of Jikoshōkai explains only the brief, factual portions of their speeches (e.g. "A soldier of love and justice! I am Sailor Moon!"). But what about the more creative parts? And why are they doing all of this on the battlefield? For that we must turn first to *jisei*, the art of Japanese death poetry," and its impact on the samurai warriors of Japan.

Jisei

Jisei are poems that are meant to be "farewell poems to life," usually reflecting the observations of the writer just prior to death. Their topics can range from the intensely personal to the oddly abstract.

The following is an example of jisei from the *Tales of Ise* :

Upon this pathway
I have long heard it said
Man sets forth at last —
Yet I had not thought to go
So very soon as today

The practice of writing jisei was not restricted to poets or artistic-minded individuals. Indeed, samurai were trained in the art of composing jisei, with the expectation that they would compose a final poetic work even in the throes of mortal agony. They were expected to do this in order to demonstrate their defiance of death and their ability to detach themselves from reality while perceiving something poetic in its structure at the moment of death.

It is this cultivated poetic skill in the Japanese warrior class that gave rise to a famous poetic exchange

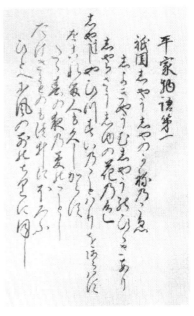

A page from the Heike Monogatari (see pg. 88)

between the legendary warriors Sadato Abe and Yoshiie Minamoto at the battle of Kawasaki in 1057 A.D.

The battle of Kawasaki

To understand why the customs of a battle in 1057 might find their way into a 1990s work like *Sailor Moon*, it is first necessary to understand the impact this confrontation had on Japanese history as a whole.

In eleventh century Japan, the Imperial Court, based in Kyoto, found itself defied by an exceptionally strong clan of samurai based in Honshu, the Abe clan. Their initial attempts to subdue this clan failed. Finally, after many years, they appointed a soldier named Yoriyoshi Minamoto to command their armies and put down the Abe clan.

Yoriyoshi and his son, Yoshiie, fought the clan for nine years. Finally, in the battle of Kawasaki, Yoshiie Minamoto confronted the leader of the Abe clan, Sadato Abe.

According to legend, in the midst of the raging battle, with their troops in mortal combat, Yoshiie drove Sadato into a corner of the battlefield, holding him at swordpoint. But instead of killing the enemy general, Yoshiie began a duel of words, reciting the last two lines of a well known poem:

> *Koromo no tate wa*
> *Hokorobinikeri*

This translates roughly to "your palace of garments has come undone at the seams." It is a clever pun, since Koromo was the name of the battleground, implying Abe's battlefield strategy had also come undone at the same time.

Sadato Abe did not miss a beat, countering with the first three lines of the poem:

> *Toshi o heshi*

Ito no midare no
Kurushisa ni

"With the long passage of time, the threads fell into disorder and could hold no longer."

Impressed by his opponent's quick reply, Yoshiie allowed Sadato to leave the battlefield with his life, claimed victory and finally put an end to the nine year war.

Although traditions of jisei poetry and jikoshōkai provide the historical substance of the introductions we see in *Sailor Moon*, they do not provide the impetus. That is found in a classic work of Japanese literature, the *Heike Monogatari* or "The Tales of Heike."

The Heike Monogatari

The *Heike Monogatari* is a 13th century account of a war between the Minamoto and Taira clans which is often cited as one of the earliest accounts of medieval Japanese battlefield tactics, and is one of the best known and widely read works of classical Japanese literature. The *Heike* records many battlefield introductions. In *The Death of Atsumori* tale, for example, we see the following exchange:

> *"Who are you? Announce your name. I will spare you," Naozane said.*
>
> *"Who are you?" The youth asked.*
>
> *"Nobody of any importance: Kumagae no Jirô Naozane, a resident of Musashi Province."*
>
> *"Then it is unnecessary to give you my name. I*

am a desirable opponent for you. Ask about me
after you take my head. Someone will recognize
me, even if I don't tell you."

"Indeed, he must be a Commander-in-Chief,"
Naozane thought.

Here we see how the concept of introductory speeches is
directly tied to battlefield etiquette and the Japanese
hierarchical class structure. Someone of "no importance" is
not worthy of being told the name of his opponent. Among
equals, such introductions are expected and, indeed, hold great
meaning. This martial custom, as depicted in one of the seminal
works of Japanese literature, likely informed the behavior of
the sailor soldiers.

In *The Tale of Tsutsui no Jomio Meishu*, another tale
in the *Heike Monogatari*, there is a description of the actions
taken by a Buddhist monk before a battle:

In a mighty voice he named his name, saying,
'You have long heard of me, now take a good
look. I am Tsutsui no Jomio Meishu, known to
all of Mii Temple as a warrior worth a thousand
men!'

This is perhaps the closest in style and tone to the introductions
used by the sailor soldiers (who describe themselves as "pretty
sailor-suited soldiers of love and justice" and then give their
names), although the sailor soldiers' introductions have evolved
considerably in form from these boasts.

While *Heike Monogatari* introductions often include
phrases which suggest that the person speaking enjoys a
certain notoriety ("known to all" as in the quote above, or, the

infamous line of *Ranma ½*'s Tatewaki Kuno: "People call me the Blue Thunder of Furinkan High!"), the characters of *Sailor Moon* rarely boast as such, usually treating each introduction as if they were just being introduced to the world.

When one considers these cultural sources—the ritual of the jikoshōkai, the poetic tradition of the samurai, and the literary legacy of the *Heike Monogatari*—it is clear that the introductory speeches of the sailor soldiers are not merely "filler" dialogue or re-introduction but rather, they are tributes to the rich culture and history from which *Sailor Moon* originates.

—*Stop right there! ...We can't forgive you... We, the Sailor Team, in the name of the moon, will punish you!*

—*Well, thanks for introducing yourselves!*
(Sailor Team to Cere-Cere)

Rei Hino: The Spirit of Japan

When manga are adapted into animated form, changes in the personalities and characteristics of the characters are often times inevitable. In the case of *Sailor Moon's* Rei Hino (Sailor Mars), the changes were dramatic—resulting in an entirely new character who sometimes shares only the most superficial attributes of her manga counterpart. These changes might irritate fans of the manga, but they shed light on some interesting Japanese cultural archetypes. The case of the "two Reis" allows us to look at two very different visions of Japanese women—the stolid, sincere *miko* (shrine maiden) of the manga, who is steeped in ancient mysticism, versus the feisty, modern, cosmopolitan miko of the anime. This also allows us to look at the way modern Japanese culture incorporates traditional elements.

The Rei Hino of the *Sailor Moon* manga is a potent symbol of ancient power and virtue. She is a quiet, reserved, young woman who takes her role as a Shinto shrine maiden quite seriously. Her psychic and spiritual abilities are well developed. She is a traditional miko who is intimately connected to the primal forces of creation. As such, despite her ethereal beauty and elegance, she has no time for relationships with men, even stating that the only lover she will ever have is the sacred flame to which she tends. She lives in the world, but is only of it as far as her obligations to school, her duties as a sailor solder, and her ties to her friends require. Manga Rei rarely loses her self control, is bluntly honest and totally dedicated—be it to her mission, her friends, her princess, her shrine, or herself. A powerful guardian-servant willing to do whatever she must to protect her charges, she inspires immediate loyalty and respect from her companions, who never doubt her motivations. She represents some of the most traditional of Japanese conceptions of the ideal woman: she is loyal, noble, and elegant.

Anime Rei, on the other hand, while still possessing the psychic abilities and position of miko of her manga counterpart, is a totally different individual. Loud-mouthed and hot-tempered, the anime's Rei Hino is indisputably modern. She dresses in the latest styles, wants to be everything from a voice actress to a successful businesswoman who trots the globe, chases boys with fearsome dedication, never hesitates to promote herself, and openly and aggressively challenges Usagi's leadership of the sailor soldiers. The fierce loyalty of her manga counterpart is less apparent, and in one episode she attempts a coup within the sailor soldiers. Worldly and aggressive, she is almost the polar opposite of her manga counterpart. Yet, she does have a few of the more traditional demure trappings that modern Japanese society demands (such as wanting to be a wonderful bride.)

The emergence of "modern Rei" in the anime is explained by the differing expectations of manga and anime audiences, as well as the different roles these forms of entertainment play in Japanese culture.

Manga and anime are vastly different art forms with different attendant genres and degrees of societal acceptance. Manga (coming out of a centuries-old genre of comic-like art) is highly regarded as an art form. Anime, for the most part, remains a "children's" medium, with the exception of sophisticated theatrical productions, or high-budget, high concept series for adults such as Masamune Shirow's *Ghost in the Shell*. The *Sailor Moon* anime is aimed at children; while some of the subtext themes are better understood by teens and adults, it is a children's show. The *Sailor Moon* manga, by contrast, was targeted at the so-called tween crowd; young adults who have generally been exposed to a wider range of ideas and concepts, can read the text, and are capable of handling more textual characters without becoming bored or confused by them. Such differences in the target audiences and their respective expectations no doubt reinforced the differences between the two Reis.

As we noted, the *Sailor Moon* anime and its cast were produced with young children in mind. The whimsical and humorous "over the top" antics of Usagi and Minako are familiar archetypes seen in many other children's shows, and generally relate to the playful, fun-loving nature of the young audience. Anime Rei constantly bickers with Usagi, and makes for great entertainment. Manga Rei, on the other hand, would have been an anachronistic element in this otherwise highly relatable mix. Her stern, severe outlook on life—which is, for want of a better term, decidedly medieval in places—would be foreign to young children. This is why, aside from her loyalty to her friends, the only characteristic Rei maintained into the anime was her status as a miko, albeit without the full exploration of the consequences of that lifestyle, as hinted at in the manga (explained in our section on religion). While children would recognize manga Rei as a "holy person," the deeper realities of her way of life, which is steeped in the ways of ancient Japan, would be lost on them, and possibly even boring to them. In contrast, Anime Rei is presented as a modern woman with modern desires and ambitions, daring to be aggressive and forward-acting. She represents, in one body, the dichotomy of modern Japan—steeped in the miko "look" of the ancient, but blazing ahead with the drive of the modern. For kids, she is "cool."

In addition, anime Rei was created by animators who were based in the neighborhood of Roppongi that was covered earlier. Having a mostly male production team, it was possible that they were more interested in having a glitzy miko from

Roppongi rather than the dull one Takeuchi wrote. Roppongi is well known for being a "red light" district with many discos, bars, and other forms of entertainment where people party late into the night. Viewed as a hot-paced, exciting area, its modern spirit and drive suffuse the character Rei on screen. But there is another part to Roppongi as well, one that is obscured by the fame and glitz of its upscale, trendy other half. Known well to Takeuchi, it is a quiet and dignified place, home to the prestigious Tōyo Eiwa Academy (where Rei goes to school). Located in an area with a plethora of embassies, it is peaceful and calm, reflecting more closely the serene nature of Manga Rei. As with the animators who gave their Rei the characteristics of the Roppongi and Japan they liked, so too did Naoko Takeuchi with *her* Rei, their two perceptions of the same city giving rise to a character whose composite is at once ancient and modern, progressive and traditional—a mirror of Japan itself and an image of its place in the modern era.

Rewriting Romeo and Juliet

In the first arc of the *Sailor Moon* manga, Takeuchi develops an allusion to Shakespeare's play *Romeo and Juliet*. Casting her characters Usagi Tsukino (Sailor Moon) and Mamoru Chiba (Tuxedo Mask) as star-crossed lovers, she connects their present fate to their lives from millennia prior, at a time when Usagi, then named Princess Serenity, was royalty of a kingdom on the moon. Mamoru too was royalty, heir apparent to the Earth and called Prince Endymion. The two celestial bodies were at war, however; manipulated by evil forces from another dimension called the Dark Kingdom.

In a flashback sequence, the reader is shown the final battle between the Earth, Moon Kingdom, and Dark Kingdom. The Dark Kingdom and Earth form an alliance and attack the

Moon. Endymion, Prince of the Earth, fights against the cause of his house and falls while attempting to protect his lover, the Moon's Princess. Following his death, the Princess takes a sword and kills herself, collapsing on top of him at the same time her Kingdom also falls.

This occurred only in the manga, however. The animators rewrote this scene, having both die at the hands of the Dark Kingdom rather than depict Princess Serenity committing suicide.

This change was made for two reasons. One, it did not match with the lighter, kid's-style fare of the animated series. The anime had a younger and far wider audience than the manga, and a suicide scene a week before the series' finale (which, in depicting the "honorable" deaths of the sailor soldiers, caused a stir across the nation, with children reported as having endured shock at seeing their favorite characters die) would have been disastrous.

The second reason has to do with the issue of youth suicide in Japan. To show the sailor soldiers killed by their enemies, as in the finale, is to depict a natural result of the folly of war. However, to have the main character, Princess Serenity (Usagi/Sailor Moon), take her own life, and to show that graphically on television, would have depicted something which the Japanese consider a social taboo. Although Westerners think of *seppuku* and *harakiri,* both a type of ritual suicide, as being part of Japanese tradition, it is considered backward by the Japanese. Suicide carries a stigma in Japan as in the rest of the world.

Furthermore, the suicide rate among teenagers in Japan is higher than the rest of the world, and headlines in the Japanese media often cause a stir among the populace. Due to bullying, ostracizing, and/or failure in school, some Japanese children and teenagers commit suicide rather than continue enduring pain from their depression. And, although it does not make headlines as frequent as youth suicides, lovers suicides (*shinjû*) are also not unheard of in Japan. The animators may not have wanted to risk blame for any suicides that could be "inspired" by the show.

Yet there is a bit of hypocrisy in the change, as told by Takeuchi herself. In a manga liner note, Takeuchi said that she did not approve of many of the changes made by the animators. Discussing the first anime season's finale, where four of the sailor soldiers are brutally murdered by the Dark Kingdom, she writes that she wanted to have the sailor soldiers die in the manga's finale as well. Her editor told her, however, "You must not kill any of your characters!"

When the anime's writers killed them, and left out the suicide flashback scene, Takeuchi "held a bit of a grudge about it." She twistedly (jokingly?) added, "I wanted to do that, too. A manga where all the characters die."

The Bells of Crystal Tokyo

The plot of the second season of *Sailor Moon* follows Tokyo's future under attack. The sailor soldiers are given a new mission: to save "Crystal Tokyo," the Tokyo of the 30th century, where Usagi reigns under the title of "Neo-Queen Serenity."

At some point in the twentieth or 21st century, the earth undergoes a disaster. The world freezes and Tokyo is in ruins, but the earth thaws, and Tokyo is rebuilt through Usagi's powers into a new utopia. Furthermore, the Azabu-Jûban district that the girls call home becomes the heart of Crystal Tokyo, the five-pointed Crystal Palace.

Not all agree with Usagi's utopian vision, however. Following the disaster that froze the earth, an evil enveloped the people of the planet. To live in the new world, they had to accept purification from Usagi; those who did not fled to the furthest reaches of the solar system. In the shadows of the planet Nemesis, they waited for their chance to return to earth. Led by the corrupt Wise Man, they come back. The Nemesians demolish Crystal Tokyo through air mines, and attempt to take the Crystal Palace.

Yet, due to the guardian powers of the 30th century sailor soldiers, the palace is impenetrable. Unable to attain their goal in the 30th century, the villains travel to the Tokyo of the early 1990s. There they attempt to corrupt the points of the Crystal Palace, so that it cannot be established in the future. The battle for the present and the future begins.

Crystal Tokyo is an archetype of the reconstructed post-apocalyptic city. This is not unique to Japanese literature, but this particular rebuilding after apocalyptic disaster is the result of a cultural imprint on the Japanese psyche: post-atomic memory. The founding of Crystal Tokyo, and the imagery of its destruction, is the cultural legacy of Hiroshima and Nagasaki.

The incendiary bombing of Tokyo in mid-March of 1945 is thought to have killed over 80,000 people and destroyed much of the downtown area, including the Minato ward in which *Sailor Moon* takes place. The Japanese government refused to capitulate following the strike, however, and American forces pressed onward toward the home islands. As spring turned into summer, the Manhattan Project that had been worked on in Los Alamos, New Mexico came to completion, and the United States government was left with a choice: risk its soldiers or use its new technology to force the Japanese into unconditional surrender.

The first atomic bomb—Little Boy—was dropped on the Japanese city of Hiroshima on August 6, 1945, and was followed three days later by a larger bomb—Fat Man—which was dropped on Nagasaki on August 9. Facing the potentiality of more atomic attacks as well as an encroaching Russian army (Russia entered the war with Japan on August 8), the Japanese government gave in to Allied demands, and the Pacific War came to a close. The war inflicted a heavy cost on the Japanese. Exhausted by fifteen years of war, the Japanese decided to work with the occupiers rather than continue their resistance. Japan entered a new era of peace, having endured the unendurable.

As the only country to have suffered an atomic bombing, Japan has been opposed to nuclear weapons ever since the end of the American occupation in 1952. This opposition, and the visual imprint of nuclear apocalypse, have seeped deep into the Japanese cultural psyche. Post-atomic themes are common in Japanese fiction, with some of the best known being the films *Godzilla* and *Akira*. The specter of nuclear war still haunts Japan, and the creation story of Crystal Tokyo, of Tokyo being completely devastated and undergoing an ice age, depends on atomic imagery.

Crystal Tokyo's creation was the result of a disaster that befell earth (something akin to attempted nuclear annihilation), causing the planet to undergo a deep freeze and to be saved by the light of Usagi's Silver Crystal. We are never told who or what caused Crystal Tokyo, though, and in the storyline it appears as an inevitability rather than something that can be stopped.

Using the power of the crystal, Usagi purifies the planet of an evil akin to the nuclear radiation that enveloped the victims of the atomic bombing. We also know that some refuse to accept her purification and flee to Nemesis, where they wait for their chance to return to earth victorious.

For some, the atomic bombing came to be considered a natural rather than man-made disaster in the sense that it was brought about by forces that could not be stopped, and that made the destruction it caused inevitable. Radiation sickness, depicted as the indescribable 'evil' that enveloped the humans in the series, was, furthermore, one of the longest lasting and most psychologically impacting events, in that many people who suffered from it were still alive to tell their stories.

Yet, while natural disasters throughout Japan's history have had horrific consequences, they are at the same time viewed as creating a "mission" for rebuilding. In his work *House and Home in Modern Japan*, Georgetown Professor Jordan Sand notes that following the 1923 earthquake that leveled much of Tokyo, some Japanese architects were almost delighted at the idea that old downtown Tokyo—with its poor planning and cramped quarters—could be rebuilt to meet modern architectural demands.[28]

This highlights a difference between Western and Japanese interpretations of atomic apocalypse. Western films portray the result of apocalypse to be a breakdown of order and the creation of a lawless wasteland; the *Mad Max* films come to mind. There are no films where New York has been completely destroyed, and then rebuilt into a technological marvel like a "New New York"; consider how the city was 'junked' in the movie *Escape From New York*. Yet many Japanese films depict a "Neo Tokyo" that has sprung up following the decimation of the old city. Other anime examples include the anime series *Bubblegum Crisis* and *Megazone 23*.

In this way, Crystal Tokyo is not a coincidental future for the series. Crystal Tokyo is the result of the sense of a "mission to rebuild" following natural disasters, and the cultural imprint of atomic apocalypse on the Japanese psyche.

Lifestyles of the Rich and Famous

Mamoru Chiba, who plays the part of "Tuxedo Mask," Sailor Moon's knight in shining armor, is the "token male" of *Sailor Moon*. He is also something of an enigma. Living alone in Tokyo with no visible means of support other than a few part time jobs, he somehow manages to cruise around the city on motorcycles and in fancy imported sports cars. Putting the question of income aside for a moment, this kind of life would not seem *that* farfetched to those of us in the West, where it is not uncommon for young college men to have either a car or a bike—and sometimes both. But *Sailor Moon* is set in Japan, and so an examination of just what it is that Mamoru has managed to construct (and further, what it would take to maintain) in his lifestyle does more than just answer some questions about his character's background—it provides a useful look into the rarely considered harsh economic and practical realities of what it means to do something as "simple" as own a car in Japan, things which Westerners generally take for granted.

Mamoru's Vehicular Expenses

Manga Mamoru has some sense. In a crowded city like Tokyo, where everything involving private transportation is expensive, he takes the bus. Maybe it is because Anime Mamoru is all grown up and in college, or maybe he just has a different mindset from his manga alter-ego, but Anime Mamoru is far less modest. Not only does he own and drive an expensive automobile, but a rare motorcycle as well. Anime Mamoru's car is an Alfa Romeo SZ and his motorcycle is a Bimota Tesi 1D—both Italian made, limited production models costing hundreds of thousands of dollars total.

An Alfa Romeo SZ.

It is unusual for someone as young as Mamoru to even *own* a car in Tokyo (let alone a foreign one), and for good reason: maintenance and associated fees are very expensive. And if you live in a big city, the traffic congestion is also discouraging. Mamoru also needs to give the motor vehicle department proof that he has a place to park his car. In Azabu-Jûban, Mamoru could expect to pay $1,000 or more each month just to park. Then there is the cost of automobile insurance, about $6,000 a year.

There are also taxes and registration fees, which together add another $1,000 a year to the cost of owning a car. The costs are so high because the car Mamoru drives is so large. There are basically two types of cars in Japan— *jōyōsha* and *kei*. Jōyōsha are larger cars, what most of us call automobiles in America. These have white license plates. Kei (meaning 'light' weight) cars, trucks, and vans have smaller engines, smaller bodies, and yellow license plates.

To purchase and maintain his car and motorcycle in real life, Mamoru would have to spend hundreds of thousands of dollars. Imagine what the frugal bus-going manga version of Mamoru would think!

Mamoru's School Expenses

Public schools in Japan are mandatory and free through middle school, but high school is not mandatory. Although there are many public schools in Japan, the elite go to private schools like Rei does. Mamoru attends private schools—the best and oldest in Tokyo.

Manga Mamoru attends Moto-Azabu Private High School. In the real Moto-Azabu area, near Azabu-Jûban, there is a school called Azabu Private Middle/High School. This is a famous school with a long history that is exceedingly difficult to get into. In the anime version, Mamoru also attends a prestigious school, Keiō University, whose main campus is located in Minato ward's Mita neighborhood.

Keiō University was founded by Yukichi Fukuzawa in 1858, and it is the oldest private university in Japan. Going to Keiō marks Mamoru as one of the best of the best. Unlike Tokyo University, whose students may work hard even in college, some regard Keiō as a place where rich kids get their degrees without working hard. Keiō is highly respected, but its students have the reputation of playboys. At points in the anime series, there are small jabs at Mamoru about this.

Not surprisingly, these elite private schools cost a bundle to attend. In early and mid-1990s monetary values and exchange rates, Mamoru's high school tuition would normally be about $6,000 per year, and his college could have been about $15,000 per year.[29] It doesn't seem a lot compared to college in America now, but it was a lot for higher education in post-economic bubble Japan.

Expense Account

In addition to his cars and education, Mamoru spends a great deal of money on other luxuries. In the manga, his collection of tuxedos is considerably large. His apartment, which is quite spacious and well stocked with technology, could further cost him thousands of dollars per month.

Living in one of the costliest wards of Tokyo, in the

most expensive district in that ward, Mamoru is the epitome of the wealthy elite. How he manages to maintain this lifestyle is a mystery, but of critical note is his attitude toward life because of it. Mamoru is very down-to-earth about his wealth, at times he could be called stingy. In one episode, after paying for a dinner that was "needed" for the mission, he chastises the sailor soldiers, telling them not to let his hard earned money go to waste.

Yet Mamoru is not the stereotypical cartoon scrooge, this is quite clear by the material possessions he owns. Instead, Mamoru represents the wealthy, intelligent elite of Tokyo, a common anime archetype. They have lots of money, which they spend on foreign cars and other goods, but they rarely dote on their wealth and are wary of being taken advantage of by others who want them to pay the restaurant bill. (Something that they always seem to end up doing.)

Two of the sailor soldiers, Haruka and Michiru (Sailor Uranus and Sailor Neptune respectively) also are archetypes of this elite. Like Mamoru, they attend expensive private high schools and live in private flats, their lives apparently disconnected from their families. (Mamoru's parents are deceased so this becomes a moot point in his case.) Although they do well in school, much of their lives are spent indulging in their hobbies of racing, painting, and music, which double as their "work."

Not Just Another Pretty Soldier

The soldier of love and beauty, Minako Aino, is a bit special in relation to her fellow sailor soldiers. From the very beginning of her days as Sailor V, her feline guardian Artemis realized there was something in her, a deeper power and potential that he just *knew* she could unleash.

The first glimmering of the power that lurks underneath Minako's sunny exterior are given in her everyday activities, which are often far "rougher" than that of the average Japanese middle school girl.

A potent aspect of Minako's character in *Sailor V* was her athletic, tomboyish disposition. The very first time we see her in *Sailor V*, Minako is involved in gymnastics. She keeps up with the boys in her class during athletic events, almost single-handedly leads her class team to victory in their autumn school festival, and even wins the Shiba Koen 35th Annual Half-Marathon. She routinely (and in an a most "unladylike" manner, according to her mother) leaps over walls to make her way home faster, more often than not dirtying her school uniform like a baseball player after a strenuous game. Not the typical teen at all!

She is the first girl to dare to enter the Crown Game Center (haven of the Japanese male species since time immemorial) unescorted, and quick to beat the established legends of the arcade, displaying her lightning-fast reflexes. This toughness and determination slowly transformed over the course of the manga and anime from mere tomboyishness (a quality that faded as Minako became more and more like the "pretty, gentle girl" she had always wanted to be) to a different kind of power, an iron will that allowed her to transcend limits most would consider inviolate.

Whatever Minako does, she does with tenacity and drive that is peerless, almost frightening. Whether destroying someone's home in order to try and clean it, two-timing in the quest for love, or staying up all night to watch over an ailing friend, Minako goes all out, "tearing along at turbo-full throttle," as she herself would put it.

The first ripples we would see of Minako's ability to do the seemingly impossible came in *Sailor V*, when, on a quest for stamps, cash, and orange juice, thirteen-year-old Minako Aino begins repeatedly donating blood beyond the bounds of human reason, while still managing to carry on her daily routine. Of course, she eventually tires out (ultimately requiring Artemis help to carry the day), but the passion with which she engaged in any activity became symbolic of her as a character.

Take, for example, when an enemy steals her "pure heart" crystal in an episode of the *Sailor Moon* anime. This followed Minako wearing herself out, having donated blood day after day (a facsimile of the manga story just mentioned); she is somehow still able to snatch the crystal back with her bare hands and run off under her own power, as she had previously bragged she would.

Minako's abilities seem to range far beyond a capacity for supernormal exertion. On more than one occasion she has shown the ability to sense things most of the other sailor soldiers cannot. In the *Sailor V* manga, Minako's "sixth sense" first begins to show as she detects raw hatred emanating from Officer Wakagi's brother (this sensing of emotion might be a side-effect of her powers as the soldier of love). She also is able to dimly detect the presence of her fellow future teammates, although the implication is this is an ability that "awoke" in her, since she had crossed their paths several times before without noticing anything out of the ordinary. In the *Sailor Moon* manga, Minako is the one who is repeatedly able to sense the presence of Sailors Uranus and Neptune before even Rei Hino, who has a highly attuned ESP.

We do not think that there is anything particularly unique to Japan about the notion of ESP being used here, except Minako is also apparently able to exorcise spirits and wield Shinto *ofuda* (pieces of paper on which a deity's name is written) in the same manner as Rei Hino does—a feat she performs *on Rei* in one of the short stories in the *Sailor Moon* manga. While it might seem odd to think that such a wild and frenetic will as Minako Aino's could be concentrated to level of intensity needed by a Shinto miko such as Rei Hino in order to accomplish such a task, when one takes Minako's previous deeds into consideration, this almost seems tame by comparison!

The tenacity with which Minako pursues her passions is often a characteristic the Japanese preserve for an *otaku*. The word is derogatory, literally meaning house, and originally referred to people who were so obsessed with things like cards and games that they rarely left their dwelling. Now the term is used to label anyone who is intense in their passions, and is generally demeaning. Minako's tomboyish and intensity are seen as something off-beat in Japanese society, where calm composure is preferred over emotion.

Idol Project

Minako Aino has a dream: to be an "idol." She does not mean she wants to be a golden calf, however. Minako, and many girls like her, dream of breaking into the Japanese starlet industry, becoming young models and amateur singers lovingly called "idols." Although America has its share of young starlets, they are people who are made famous for having an exceptional ability that puts them above the pack. Japanese idols, however, are never so exceptional that they seem too "far" away; one of the notable attributes of a Japanese idol is that she is just 'normal' enough to elicit feelings that her fans could someday meet her and become her friend (or boyfriend).

The career of most idols is short and runs at breakneck speed. Many will reach the height of their stardom in their teens, and from the time their first CD comes out to the time that CD is in the dust bin could be less than a year. Many are also highly exploited, releasing provocative picture books and DVDs of themselves in bathing suits and bikinis, prancing around for the benefit of the viewer. Although most of these DVDs are innocent in their nature insofar as there is nothing more than a girl splashing around on the beach, the age of the star may be as low as nine years old, and these DVDs might be considered child pornography in other countries.

That everyone wants to be a star, and may do anything to that end, is the dark side to the idol industry. *Sailor Moon* has critiqued it in several ways. In the *Sailor V* manga, the Dark Agency uses the industry to gain money and serve their nefarious purposes. Villains in the *Sailor Moon* anime are also fond of taking advantage of idols and people wanting a quick path to fame. In an early episode of the first season, entitled *Usagi's Reconsideration: The Road to Stardom is Tough*, the villain Jadeite watches an idol perform and comments that the desires of the people watching her would make for abundant energy. He has a demon impersonate the idol and holds a fake contest, which many people fall for.

Luckily, most idols do not have to worry about walking into demonic traps. And many will not follow the exploitation road. Despite the difficult path of an idol, it is worth the risks to most because a few of them will break out of the idol mold and become full-fledged stars in Japanese television and cinema. Given the short nature of most idol careers, the majority of idols do not want to remain idols for long, lest their star fade and they become forgotten. But debuting as an idol is one of the only paths to becoming genuinely famous, and it is for this reason that girls like Minako are willing to forget the unpleasant side of things and focus on the benefits: an audience of adoring fans chanting your name.

Minako does not just sit around and practice being an

idol; Artemis refers to her at one point as an *oikake* or "chaser"; someone who follows around idols obsessively, as their seikatsu. Calling someone an oikake is not a compliment, as it implies that they are pretty pathetic in their obsession. Negative tone aside, the term idol chaser seems to fit Minako very well. Not only does she want to be a star, but she loves hanging around them as well. In the fifth season of *Sailor Moon* she attempts to become the assistant of the singing trio *Three Lights*, partially because she loves them as stars, but also so she can be seen around them and potentially be discovered.

Incidentally, one particular idol success story has been a major influence on the *Sailor Moon* series from the very beginning. Naoko Takeuchi apparently lifted Ami's good looks from a real idol; the character of Ami Mizuno, according to notes included in the *Materials Collection* book, is actually based on a famous Japanese idol named Noriko Sakai.

Born on Valentine's Day in 1971, Sakai debuted at the age of 16 with her first album, "Fantasia," and quickly became a big star. Unlike most idols, who fizzle out after one or two albums, she has remained a major figure in the music and modeling circuit to this very day, with dozens of albums and singles in her discography.

How closely does Ami resemble Sakai? While Sakai's looks and style have changed drastically over the decades the album she released in mid-1991 (a few months before *Sailor Moon* debuted) called *Sentimental Best* has her on the cover with a striking resemblance to Ami's hairstyle and facial features.

Haruka Ten'ō's Gender Crisis?

In the manga, Haruka Ten'ō (Sailor Uranus) is often drawn as a male, with masculine proportions. People on the street—not to mention Usagi and Mamoru—routinely mistake her for a "him." This, coupled with the cryptic comment of her partner Michiru Kaiō (Sailor Neptune) in an act of the manga (ironically intended to *clear up* Usagi's confusion regarding Haruka's gender) that "Uranus is both a man and a woman. A soldier of both genders, with the strengths and personalities of each," engendered much dismay among followers of the manga, even causing some to speculate that Haruka was hermaphroditic! (It would not be unusual for the series, this indeed *was* the case for the Sailor Starlights, and Takeuchi herself had toyed with the notion of making the villainous Amazon Trio be creatures of both genders.) Takeuchi added to the confusion by having Haruka say things in the manga like, "A man, a woman... is it that important [what I am]?"

Because of such lines, Takeuchi has had to address this point many times over the years. In an interview published in an issue of Germany's *AnimaniA* magazine, she clarified the issue and provided some insight on Haruka's origins and the reason Haruka was even included in the manga in the first place:

> *Characters like Haruka, these tough masculine women, a little like the actresses who portray men in* takarazuka *theater, are fundamentally and extremely popular in Japan, especially with the female public. They embody the best female friend and the fairy tale prince in one, so to speak. I've long wanted to incorporate such a character into one of my works.*

As Takeuchi noted, Japan has had a tradition of female actresses portraying men in theater revues (*takarazuka*), and the Haruka character is a reflection of that tradition: she is a strong, female character who often dresses like a man.

Using a takarazuka-style character matches with Takeuchi's audience, the young adolescent female, perfectly. As anthropologist Jennifer Robertson has studied in her book of the same title, *Takarazuka*, the revues are glitzy theatrical productions widely popular among *young women*. Takeuchi's fan base, similar in age and gender to that of those who attend the revues, adore the character.[30]

This also explains the behavior of Makoto Kino (Sailor Jupiter) in one episode of the anime. Idolizing Haruka, Makoto goes on a psuedo-date with her, and the other girls gossip as to whether Makoto has a crush. By the end of the episode, we find that Makoto was not in love with Haruka, but rather, that she saw in Haruka the woman Makoto wanted to be: "cool."

On another note, *Sailor Moon* as a production could be a reflection of a different theater tradition, that of *kengeki* or "swordplay" theater. Edward Seidensticker notes in his book *Tokyo Rising* of past kengeki performances,

> *Female swordplayers . . . brought in eroticism, as the men could not easily do. Like plucky little Orientals overwhelming huge ugly Occidentals in Bruce Lee movies, they were always overcoming adversaries more muscular than they, and they appealed to the sympathy for the underdog which was a part of the image the son of Edo and Tokyo had of himself. Best of all, they managed, wielding their swords, to show their legs every bit as generously as the review girls were permitted to do.[31]*

Overcoming large adversaries and a bit of eroticism are staples of the series. And although the sailor soldiers do not rely upon them, swords appear frequently in the *Sailor Moon* manga. Haruka herself carries a sword in the anime.

Education

There is a popular stereotype, especially in America, of the Japanese student as focused, dedicated, and above all, extremely studious. What this preconception fails to take into consideration, however, are the social and cultural pressures that lead to this kind of behavior. Japanese students spend 240 days a year at school, 60 days more than their American counterparts. This includes, for some schools, half days on Saturdays (until 2003), and school days that routinely last into the evening. For these students—assuming they want to "be anything" in life—studying to excess is critically important.

Sailor Moon, unlike many manga/anime series that gloss over the hard realities of a teenage girl's educational life, takes a direct look at the often torturous educational system. This occurs often through the lens of the "genius girl" character of Ami Mizuno (Sailor Mercury), whose obsessive-compulsive study habits make her the embodiment of the Japanese student stereotype. What makes *Sailor Moon* an especially valuable resource in examining Japanese education is the diversity of the characters and their educational experiences. Through these characters, we can learn more about the pressures children must endure to succeed in modern Japanese society.

Ami's debut episode of the anime makes clear that her school life is a commentary on the Japanese educational system. At the start of the episode, the anime's two villains, Queen Beryl and General Jadeite, break character and describe the system of education in Japan:

Jadeite: *The children of Japan are pushed into*

studying all the time.

Beryl: *I hear there are women called 'education mothers' who are as fierce as demons.*

Jadeite: *They are extremely desperate to have their children get in first rated kindergartens, first rated elementary schools, first rated secondary schools, the best high schools and the top universities.*

Beryl: *And what will become of them after graduating the top universities?*

Jadeite: *That I do not know.*

As this dialogue illustrates, Japanese schools work different than American schools, where education through the high school level is open to all by simply passing from one grade to the next. In both Japan and the United States, the distinguishing factor on someone's *curriculum vitae* comes from what university one attends. But in Japan, what one takes at the university level is less critical, university instead being a place where one can "coast," parlaying the way into work afterwards with relative ease. In America, however, students must work hard even through college.

Perhaps the main difference lies at the high school entrance level. To get into the best colleges in Japan, a student usually has to attend one of the best high schools. But to attend the best high schools they must pass an entrance examination, which they begin preparing for in middle school, and which we see the girls studying for in the first four seasons of *Sailor Moon*.

These tests, for both the high school and college level, are demanding written examinations on Japanese language, mathematics, science, social studies, and English. To pass them requires great independent study beyond the pale of the subjects offered in standard education up to that stage. This is why, the first time we see her, Ami Mizuno is attending the "Crystal Seminar," a special school for after school hours called a *juku*.

Juku Journey

A *juku* is a "cram" school that students go to after their regular school hours for several days a week. About 60% of students in Japan attend juku well into the evening to further their education. In addition to preparing students academically for the subjects that will be covered on their examinations, these schools can also offer non-academic lessons covering topics like art and calligraphy, serving to broaden the range of what a student can learn beyond the barebones prefectural educational requirements. For someone like Ami, who has a strong drive to do well and become a doctor, juku is a necessity.

Over the short real-time span of the series, we see Ami attend "OK! Going to College Juku," "You Definitely Will Succeed Juku," and "Number 1 Seminar School." The names seem rather silly in English, but highlight another important cultural difference. While Westerners might scoff at such "cheesy" names, in Japan, those kinds of direct, emphatic titles sell. After all, one would not want to go to a school called "Hey we might be able to get you into college kinda juku"! (It is worth noting that as a testament to her character's genius nature, Ami seems to go to juku for *high schoolers* preparing for college entrance exams, rather than the ones for middle schoolers preparing for high school.)

With her high ranking on national mock exams and her high IQ, Ami is something of a minor celebrity in academic circles. The people who run the Crystal Seminar, the juku we see her attend in her debut episode, knew that her attendance would boost their profile tremendously. Given the intense competition between students, those who are driven to excellence would make it their business to find out what juku Ami goes to—this is reflected in the "Mercury vs. Mercurius" battle in the *Ami's First Love* special, where, tired of being tied for first place on exams with the mysterious "Mercurius," Ami hunts down his juku and decides to attend it. Juku are known to exploit these competitive tendencies to great commercial effect. And this serves to highlight another real-world trait of the juku—their blatantly commercial nature.

Juku is not free. They are for-profit, after-school programs, and they are expensive. But they may have been offering Ami incentives such as free attendance and special study privileges, because juku depend on their high school pass rates to gain students—they thus advertise aggressively. In the anime, the Crystal Seminar uses Ami's image on its advertising. Usagi's friend Umino states that Ami is on the "preferred students list" for the seminar and gets to attend for free. The implication, therefore, is that the seminar pushed for her attendance, allowing her to attend the juku for free in order to attract more clients.

The fact that students who wish to succeed academically must attend an expensive juku has come under criticism. Some commentators have written that the Japanese school system, instead of educating its students, is designed solely to instill in them a Japanese ideal of respect of authority. For example, schools encourage students to join clubs in which they are first brought in as subservient *kohai* (lower ranked students) beholden to the privilege and tutelage of the *senpai* (upperclassmen). Because the regular schools do not teach what is on the entrance examinations, kids are *forced* to attend juku, which is where the "real" learning happens—and only at a steep financial cost.

Minako (Sailor Venus) is a good example of a typical Japanese student affected by this policy. In the *Sailor V* manga, Minako attends a juku named "Glory Cram School." Unlike Ami, she does not go for free. Also unlike Ami, Minako does not like to study. Yet she goes to cram school. Why? We see a telling scene in the manga where her mother pressures her to make something of herself, so that she does not end up in a dead-end job like her father. While Ami represents the scholar who learns for learning's sake, Minako represents the average Japanese child, who is pushed to advance by getting into a good high school via a juku education.

Usagi does not attend a cram school at all. The "anti-Ami," Usagi has a single goal: to get married. She wants a prince to ride in and sweep her away in a typical storybook romance. Thus, she spends very little time on her own pursuing educational goals. Without the help of the other girls, it is unlikely Usagi would have managed to get into Jûban High School.

Her character illustrates the cost of not attending juku in Japan. Future Usagi is portrayed as a woman who only writes in *hiragana* and *katakana*, the two simplest syllabaries of the Japanese language. Her ability to use *kanji* (Chinese ideograms), which denote a more advanced vocabulary and intellectual development, is repeatedly shown to be nonexistent. Were it not for history placing Usagi at the summit of power in the distant future, it is likely she would have ended up in some menial, low class job (although odds are she'd become a homemaker.)

Indeed, in perhaps what is yet another series commentary on Japanese education, Usagi's high school success is a tribute to the "peer pressure" nature of Japanese society. She succeeds because her friends expect her to succeed, reflecting the Japanese belief that all students have roughly the same capacity to succeed, with the personal motivation of the student being the only limiting factor. This is different from American conceptions of educational handicaps, which sometimes lead people to assume there are genetic or cultural differences for academic successes or failures. The American solution is to create an even playing field by busing minorities to different school districts, or, at the college level, create different entrance requirements for some groups.

In contrast, the Japanese solution chastises the individual for failing to be motivated. But this also means that the solution to success, as seen in *Sailor Moon*, is perseverance. Usagi's friends *never*, despite their frustrations, give up on her. With her guardian feline Luna's pressure on her to read, Ami's pressure on Usagi to study, as well as Mamoru's help, Usagi actually has a number of intelligent people from whom to learn. For the typical Japanese student, however, their course is more likely to be that of Ami's minus the friendship and free study courses—an expensive, time-consuming, difficult and necessary journey towards success.

Religion

*J*apanese society has been called areligious. Many Japanese will suggest that theirs is a society in which religious practices such as weekly church gatherings and a belief in an all-powerful God play no part in daily life. But to call this areligious assumes Western religious practices to be the universal measure of religion. Insofar as beliefs and rites relating to the spiritual exist and are practiced, Japan is very much a religious society.

Two religions have dominated Japan's cultural landscape: Buddhism, which arrived in Japan via China and Korea, and Shintoism, a religion unique to the Japanese archipelago. Throughout the reign of the Tokugawa Shogunate (1603-1868), Buddhism was of primary official patronage. Tokugawa Shoguns were buried using Buddhist rites and in Buddhist temples, and the religion prospered under their watch. Shintoism would have its day following the restoration of the Emperor to power in 1868, and became the official "religion" of Japan through the end of World War II, when it lost its government support.

These categories are just on the official landscape of religious regulation, however. The average Japanese throughout history has seen little difference between a Shinto shrine and a Buddhist temple, and even some priests practice syncretism, which sees lines between the two religions blurred. Instead of having concrete distinctions, the two religions blend into each other in mythology and practice, sometimes making one of little consequence as an alternative over the other to the lay practitioner.

Take, for instance, an episode of *Sailor Moon* in which Sailor Jupiter flees to a Buddhist temple in the mountains. Unlike the monk from whom she gains wisdom, she is not devoted to, nor even knowledgeable about, the temple's religious practices. She simply desires a quiet place to train her body and mind, which she had heard that temple was known for. It could have been a Shinto shrine, or even a church; that it was a Buddhist temple made little difference to her.

This is not to suggest, however, that Buddhism and Shintoism are interchangeable. They have very different concerns and outlooks on life. Buddhism focuses on the attaining of nirvana, and has a strict moral code. Shintoism focuses its followers on reverence of spirits and ancestors, lacks a moral code, and has no canon. As depicted in *Sailor Moon* by the gaggle of school girls flocking to Rei Hino's (Sailor Mars) Hikawa shrine to buy charms after school, many young Japanese are not concerned with either religions' ultimate goal. They will toss in coins for the good fortune of a Buddhist deity, or head to a Shinto shrine to purchase a protective amulet in a desire for better luck.

While these casual purchases make up the bulk of a Shinto shrines' income, without a regular congregation it is sometimes difficult for shrines and temples to make ends meet. They must instead rely on the generosity and vapid interests of the local population. Rei's grandfather knows this, and he is willing to go to odd ends—such as opening a women's wrestling gym—to find financial support for the shrine and draw people to it for something other than just their weekly amulet. Despite the declining relevance of Shinto to peoples' lives, however, Shinto shrines remain an important part of the local community, particularly in the running of annual festivals, as we shall see.

Shrine Goddess

Rei Hino is a *miko* or Shinto shrine maiden. What exactly is a shrine maiden, however? What is it that she *does*, apart from sweep the grounds and sell dainty love charms?

Shinto scholar C. Scott Littleton considers Shinto to be the *lifestyle* of the Japanese people rather than the religion of Japan. What we would think of as typical elements of a religion, like a plan for the afterlife, worship of an immortal figure or figures, and theological discussions, are not part of Shintoism. Rather, Shinto, which literally means *way of the kami* (kami means 'spirits'), is characterized by a belief in natural spirits, ancestral respect, family ties, and a strong connection to Japan as a living land where the sun goddess was born. Local shrines also serve as social gathering places and village centers. With the Meiji restoration of the late nineteenth century, which set Japan on its path to modernization, Shinto was harnessed and used as a way to commonly unite the people under the Emperor (who is, in Shinto myth, the direct descendent of the sun goddess).[32]

Shinto priests do not hold services or give sermons but they perform rituals for the community, particularly those of purification. They are called upon to ward off evil spirits when building a new house, for example. Both men and women can become Shinto priests, and priests are allowed to marry and have children. (Often a shrine will be kept by a single family and this is the only way it can continue to be supported.) But Rei is not a priestess; she is a miko.

A miko is a shrine maiden who assists the priest in purification rituals, performs sacred dances, and sells *ofuda* and charms. Ofuda are pieces of paper on which the shrine's deity's name is written. These are typically taken home and placed in a family's alter, but Rei uses hers to ward off evil spirits.

In general, miko are the priest's daughters, and it is important to note that a miko must be unmarried in order to wear the traditional white kimono. Unless she takes the full priest position, she cannot both get married and continue to be a miko. However, a woman can cease being a miko, get married and have children, and later resume her duties *if* she purifies herself by remaining chaste for a certain number of years (and, of course, continuing afterwards).

In the anime, Rei's attitude toward boys is completely different from that in the manga—here she *plans* to fall in love and get married. It comes as no surprise, then, that she treats her miko position as only a part-time job which she will not continue to do when she is older. Manga Rei, however, has no plans to fall in love or get married, and will likely continue to be a miko her entire life.

In addition, as a miko, Rei is required to perform a complex ceremonial dance known as the *Kagura*. The word Kagura translates to "place of the gods," but the characters that make up the word literally mean "music of the gods." The term refers to a performance involving music and dance celebrating the renewal of life, and the ceremony traces itself back to the very roots of Japanese myth. In those myths, the sun goddess, Amaterasu Okami, was lured out of hiding by a dance performed by the goddess Ama no Uzume no Mikoto. This led to a belief that dances such as the Kagura pacified the ancient gods, consoled them, and offered them entertainment.

While it can be done in public, this dance, which is performed much the same way as it has been for two thousand years, is traditionally performed by several miko in austere settings, where no one but the performers can see what goes on. The form of the Kagura dance hearkens back to the era in which such miko were not mere subordinates to a temple priest, but rather shamans in their own right. The swaying motions of the dance, together with rhythmical stamping and hand-raising, all look back to a time when a miko would seek to induce a trance state in which she offers her body for possession by the deities, who would then convey their messages through her. Some of these miko, known as *aruki miko*, would go from one village to the next, dancing and passing along their messages. The dance of the aruki miko actually served as the basis for a better known form of Japanese theatre, Kabuki, and is sometimes performed by lay practitioners in the local festival.

Festival of Fire

In a memorable episode of the third season of the *Sailor Moon* anime, Rei takes charge of the local Jûban festival or *matsuri*, using her talents to turn it into a rousing success. The writers of the episode using Rei as the manager of the festival makes logical sense given Rei's miko position.

Rei mentions that her grandfather's friend asked her to join the *Committee to Make the Jûban Festival More Exciting*. While this sounds strange, it was actually fairly common at the period. In addition, as one of those in charge of the Azabu Hikawa shrine, her grandfather and his family would be expected to be involved in the festival.

The Jûban summer festival in the anime resembles the Summer's Eve festival that normally occurs in Jûban every year in August, when this episode originally aired. While the real festival focuses on the various embassy booths, it shares many characteristics with typical urban festivals. Those festivals are run in conjunction with the local Shinto shrine—in this case, the Hikawa shrine, since it is the biggest in the area. While the Jûban festival in the show is not a Shinto festival, in a regular Tokyo community festival, the shrine provides the focal point for the festival's organization. The committees that set up the festival are staffed by both local leaders and those involved with the shrine, and they help to make the festival come alive.

The festival in a Japanese urban district tends to have dual purposes: it brings the community together under a common banner, and promotes the shrine and businesses. Festivals are incredibly popular, but require a lot of planning (committees for next year's festival are usually set up right after the current year's festival ends). In this *Sailor Moon* festival episode, we see traditional booths that are set up at many festivals, including Minako's goldfish scooping booth.

In the show, Rei and her friends man these booths. In real life, however, they are typically the domain of professional festival booth troupes, sometimes belonging to the Japanese mafia (*yakuza*). This is depicted in the series as well. In another festival episode in the fourth season of the *Sailor Moon* anime, we see a gruff old man running a balloon booth. He allows one of the characters to give away his balloons, thinking she will pay him. When he discovers she lacks money, one of the season's villains intervenes. In a comical scene, the old man beats him up, speaking yakuza slang, for not paying for her.

The trend since the 1980s has been toward reinvigorating urban festivals, which had declined after World War II. Committees such as the one Rei joined to "make the festival more exciting" were typical in many other Tokyo neighborhoods at the time, as they were concerned about their festivals losing support. Some would try to raise money to buy fancy new *mikoshi* (the arks that are carried around during a festival which contain the local shrine's deity inside), and others attempted to bring in traditional attractions, such as the famous *taiko* drum player Maya Tōno that Rei sought to recruit for her festival.

The Kuji
Rei's Claim to Fame

There are many instances in *Sailor Moon* where Rei Hino consults the sacred flame at the Hikawa Shrine in order to gain deeper insight into the nature of an enemy or crisis that has arisen. Before and during her meditations on the flame, she performs a Shinto ceremony that involves the use of several complex hand motions and incantations. This is a Shinto practice known as the *kuji* (literally "the nine characters").

The kuji's roots are in Chinese Taoism (alchemy) and it was handed down to Japan together with fortune telling. It was developed as a ritual to ward against evil by the followers of an ascetic practice called *Shugendō,* which was a form of mountain asceticism-shamanism that incorporated Shinto and Buddhist concepts.

The kuji incantation itself is a Buddhist war chant. A large, frightening figure appears on the screen during Rei's incantation of this ceremony, and he is the god of war from Buddhist lore. Since Rei is a Shintoist and not a Buddhist (and according to one episode, considers the other religions her "competition") the display of a Buddhist god is a contemporary example of syncretism we discussed earlier, which blurs Shintoism and Buddhism for most Japanese (in this case, the anime's writers).

In *Sailor Moon*, the method of the kuji that Rei Hino performs involves tying a "pledge seal" with her fingers via various hand motions. This style was said to have been designed by the founder of Japan's *Kōbōdaishi* ("true word") religious sect, Kûkai.

The kuji is normally performed like this (from top left to bottom right):

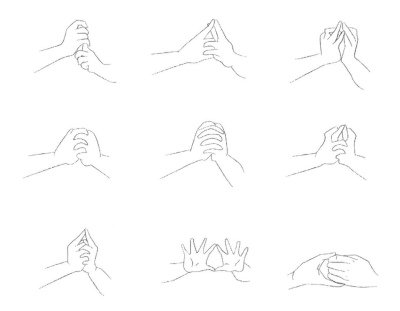

First, the "*kongō gasshō*" is performed, with the hands joined together in a diamond-like shape.

Then, the prayer "*namu honzon ekai, marishiten rairin e kou sono kō mamorashi meta mai*" ("Hail the very boundary of understanding, give me protection on behalf of facing the image of Marici") is recited. Marici is a Buddhist god of war. The next step is to "tie" the nine pledge seals by performing the hand motions whilst reciting their various names.

Typically the Shinto practitioner will have mastered each of these nine *shutō* (hand swords)—via meditation and contemplation—before performing the ceremony. Together the nine seals make up what is called the *kuji no in*. Should you have mastered them, and if you have been able to unify your body and mind in the process (a key Buddhist concept), you are then able to use the "tenth sign" method, which is even more powerful. A tenth character is 'cut' into the center of the grid, but changes depending on circumstances. For example, if the practitioner were sick, he or she would put the appropriate kanji character in there. If being attacked and wanting protection, he or she would use a different character.[33]

Instead of her hand signals, Rei sometimes does this motion with her ofuda (a of paper with a deity's name written on it). In these situations, she traces out a grid in the air, traveling from the upper left while alternating the horizontal and vertical motions; turning and moving to the right horizontally, switching direction as the cuts are called out until the whole grid is completed.

Endymion's Sword

In the Japanese context, syncretism usually refers to the blending of Buddhist and Shinto beliefs. However, Japanese also make frequent use of Christian iconography and imagery, particularly the cross, but without the rhetorical weight of the original context. For an example, we turn to the third *Sailor Moon* arc, where *Sailor Moon* was referred to as the "Messiah." While it is tempting to seize upon this use of Christian symbolism (which also includes the use of such Western religious icons as churches, crosses, and, not least of all, the holy grail) as evidence of a theological meaning behind the third season of *Sailor Moon,* as with most Japanese uses of Christian symbols, this is not the case.

Kuniko Ikuhara, director of the third season of *Sailor Moon*, has said that "[the anime makers] had no intention of meaningfulness in the religious references that appear in *Sailor Moon.* The country of Japan is areligious. To the views of most Japanese people, religious references are not too different from fantastical elements. [The elements] were not added because of [a desire to indicate religious] devotion."

The Japanese use of Western religious symbols is generally secular, having little to do with the underlying beliefs that originally gave rise to them. Take, for instance, the Christian holiday of Christmas. While Christmas is a major holiday in Japan, complete with lit trees, cameos from Santa Claus, and frenetic shoppers just as in the West, it bears no connection to its Western meaning as a celebration of the birth of Jesus. Similarly, in the third season the sailor soldiers are looking for the "Messiah of Light." To the western mind, the word "Messiah" generally conjures up images of a Jesus figure; but not necessarily to the Japanese.

In *Sailor Moon*, "Messiah" has not kept its Western meaning; as with many foreign loanwords, it has been redefined to symbolize a much more generic concept. Rather than referring to a "deliverer of the Israelites" (the original Greek definition of "Christ"), the meaning of "Messiah" is generalized, becoming "a person who would reflect the will of the heavens."

Similarly, the use of a cross in both the second season of *Sailor Moon* (on an enemies' spaceship) and the third season (where Sailor Neptune is crucified) is not a direct reference to Jesus. Instead, it is an abstract symbol depicting a connection between the sailor soldiers and higher, godlike powers that the typical Japanese person, only casually acquainted with the "meaning" of a Christian cross, could easily grasp. Although it should be noted that crucifixion existed in Japan before Christianity's entrance, in *Sailor Moon* it was most likely meant to be tied to the Christian context of being "holy." When questioned about the "crucifixion" scene in the third season, director Kuniko Ikuhara said, "[Neptune] looked good crucified, so we crucified her. Christ is an object of religious fantasy in Japan, so that is how it was used. He is just another character in fantasy to us. Even if references to crucifixion were made in *Sailor Moon*, it was not as part of an attempt to communicate a religious message."

This kind of varied symbolism can be seen in the average American viewer's conception of individuals and objects related to the practice of Shinto, such as shrine *miko*, *ofuda*, temples and sacred flames. While most viewers would superficially understand their association with "good" things (shrine *miko* are obviously "holy" people who banish evil and engage in other "holy" tasks), a deeper understanding of the implications of everything shown—from the reasons for the upward-curving shapes of temple roofs to the meaning behind the often-seen slips of white paper tied to tree limbs—would be completely lacking.

So, what does this non-Judeo-Christian "Messiah" represent? Taking into consideration a variety of facts about the Silver Millennium (the Moon Kingdom in which Usagi's first incarnation lived) from *Sailor Moon*'s first season, the kingdom on the moon during the Silver Millennium was a type of "heaven" and her magical Silver Crystal and Moon Palace beacons of holy light.

The Greek myth of Selene and Endymion provided Naoko Takeuchi the basis for much of *Sailor Moon*'s mythology. In the Greek myth, Selene was the moon goddess who captured the heart of the earthling Endymion and put him into an eternal sleep so she could keep him on the moon forever. In *Sailor Moon*, Usagi as "Princess Serenity," a play on the name Selene, was also a moon goddess to the people of earth, and fell in love with the earth's Prince Endymion (Mamoru Chiba). During the time of the Silver Millennium, the people of earth had looked up to the people of the moon, who were tasked with helping the humans on the world below.[34]

Thus, the Messiah in *Sailor Moon* was an angel from the heavens who had come to save the earth. Indeed, Usagi, as Sailor Moon, frequently displays an angel motif. In many of her transformation sequences, Sailor Moon is seen sporting angel wings. At the end of the fourth season, she and her daughter both float to earth as winged beings. In the fifth season her "Eternal" form has faux wings, and in her final showdown with the evil incarnate Galaxia, she wears nothing *but* her wings.

From there, it is only a small leap to say that the "Messiah" concept refers to Usagi as a "savior." This is reinforced by the depiction of the future, Crystal Tokyo, in the second season, when she purifies the world after its corruption. It is also worth noting that, after using the third season's "Holy Grail," Sailor Moon's attack features images of the Silver Millennium.

Western mythological and theological concepts are not the only ones featured in the third season of *Sailor Moon*; traditional Japanese legend plays a prominent role. Three sought after Talismans are actually representations of sacred objects known as the *Shinki,* which are related to the Japanese myth of the world's creation. According to the legend, Japan is the birthplace of Amaterasu Okami (the sun goddess; hence the Japanese rising sun flag). In the story of Japan's birth, Amaterasu's brother, Susanō no Mikoto, angers his sister by misbehaving. Enraged by his actions, Amaterasu, the sun, goes into hiding in a cave. To make up for his mistake, Susanō saves the Princess Kushiinada (who was to be sacrificed to the eight-headed dragon *Yamata no Orochi*) by beheading the dragon. He in turn finds the Kusanagi sword in its tail. Susanō lures his sister out of the cave she had been hiding in by using a mirror and gives her the sword he had obtained; in return, as thanks for the sword and in recognition of his deeds, Amaterasu gives him special jewels. Later, when Amaterasu's descendant Jimmu arrives on earth, Amaterasu gives him the sword, mirror, and jewels and Jimmu becomes the first emperor of Japan. The Shinki are considered royal emblems; the sword is located at the Atsuta shrine and the mirror at the Ise shrine. You can visit both shrines in Japan.

In *Sailor Moon*, Takeuchi used all three of the Shinki as "Talismans" which three sailor soldiers—Uranus, Neptune, and Pluto—were charged with finding and protecting. The Kusanagi sword became Sailor Uranus's Space Sword, the mirror became Sailor Neptune's Aqua Mirror, and the jewels became Sailor Pluto's Garnet Jewel. Combined, the three items heralded the creation of the New Testament's "Holy Grail"; an interesting mix of Christian and Japanese myths.

Very little of the show's Japanese audience, however, could be expected to understand to the allusion to the New Testament. Thus, for Japanese fans, this all came down to the familiar battle between good and evil that is easily recognizable in the mythology of all cultures.

The anime's director, Ikuhara, may not have intended to infuse the season with religious meaning, but Takeuchi had background in mythology and researched myths extensively in preparing her stories. However, her target audience was young Japanese girls, who could not be expected to know these mythological details, and so Takeuchi used them to give her characters an air of heavenly purpose.

Both of their uses of Christian theological elements were not to make Sailor Moon seem as stand-in for Jesus any more than Sailor Jupiter could be a direct replacement for Jupiter, the Roman god of Thunder—it was simply to provide *Sailor Moon* with a sense of mythical depth and historical connection.

Foreign Influences

*W*e discussed in the "Religion" chapter the practice of religious syncretism in Japan. But syncretism can be a broader concept than just a blurring of religions; it can also refer to a crossing of beliefs that creates a third, quasi-hybrid phenomenon. A mix of East and West occurs in Japan without reservation. *Sailor Moon* is an excellent example of such cross-pollination at work in Japanese popular culture.

Naoko Takeuchi's extensive study of Western astrology and myth has allowed for a rich tapestry which imbues her work with a deep, cross-cultural significance. To see this at work, one need look no further than the fact that the sailor soldiers are clad in variants of Japanese sailor suits, which were originally adopted as a school standard from British sailor uniforms, and that they go by the names of ancient Roman gods and goddesses, yet employ attack powers that stem from a mixture of Eastern and Western astrological influences.

This is but one example of how Japan has borrowed ideas from many civilizations and remade them in a uniquely Japanese way. For another example, we will be discussing shortly the Japanese practice of blood-type divination and its role in the development of the sailor soldiers' personalities. A person's blood type was a discovery of Western science, and divination an ancient Chinese practice. The two were combined in Japan to make a *new* type of fortune telling that is unique to Japan both in practice and in popularity.

The Japanese easily mix Western and Eastern styles, and have been doing so ever since opening up to foreign influence in the mid-nineteenth century. Following the Meiji restoration of 1868 a popular catchphrase became *wakon yōsai*: Japanese spirit, Western learning. This concept applied not just to industry and the military, but to Japanese *seikatsu* or "lifestyle" as well. Even people's homes at the turn of the twentieth century were built fusing Western exterior architecture with Chinese feng shui and Japanese traditional interior design. Modern Japan, it could be said, is a country built on practices of mixing East and West. *Sailor Moon* makes for an excellent—and deceptively simple—candidate for analysis on these lines.

Moonlight Magic

Astrological references—both Oriental and Occidental—play a major part in *Sailor Moon*, from providing the basis for the sailor soldiers' backgrounds and attacks, to defining rough contours of their birthdates and personalities. The soldiers are named after the Roman mythological gods and goddesses that have given their names to our planets, but the girls' powers come from another borrowed system, that of the five elements of Chinese cosmology.

Early designs of Usagi's transformation brooch lend themselves to astrological analysis. The first brooch has a crescent moon and a sun-like spherical circle in it. Going clockwise around the brooch are red, yellow, blue, and green, tiny jewel-like objects which are studded into it. These jewels correspond with Sailor Mars, Sailor Venus, Sailor Mercury, and Sailor Jupiter's respective colors. These colors also happen to represent the five elements in Chinese cosmology that compose all of space: Wood, Fire, Earth, Metal, and Water, and after which the Japanese names of the planets are called. Mercury in Japanese is *suisei* or water star, Mars is *kasei* or fire star, Jupiter is *mokusei* or wood star, and Venus is *kinsei* or gold star. In Oriental astrology, the Moon and Sun each respectively represent yin (negative power) and yang (positive power) and united in the ying-yang form they represents the planet earth as a whole.

In addition to having the five soldiers' elemental colors represented on the brooch, the brooch hints at the origin points for the soldiers' attack styles. To begin with, Sailor Mercury, with her blue image color, uses water based attacks like Shabon Spray (a mist-based attack), and her color is associated with ice. It should be noted that there are two five-elements theories, the original created thousands of years ago, and a 'revamped' version which is slightly more recent. The difference relevant to us is that in the original theory, water was represented by the color black, and is now blue.

Represented by the red imagery of flames is Sailor Mars, whose corresponding deity planet Mars is represented by fire in both Western and five-elements theories. This works out well for her, as fire is her specialty. As was noted earlier, the Hikawa shrine she is connected to is not actually related to fire. They are, in fact, ice shrines. Their character was changed to fire to match Mars better.

Sailor Jupiter's Supreme Thunder (an electric attack) and Flower Hurricane (a plant/wind attack) are represented in five-elements theory by the planet Jupiter, the wood star. Makoto, given her disposition toward wood, has a particular love of plants, and her hobbies include gardening. This covers Oriental mythology, but Zeus, or Jupiter, was the god of lightning, so certainly the Roman reflection is an appropriate interpretation of her powers too.

Yellow is the color of gold and the signal color of Venus, many of whose attacks feature prominent yellow/gold imagery. In five-elements theory, gold is indicative of metal because the characters that spell gold have the character for metal in them.

But yellow is also the color of earth, the centerpiece of the five elements, and in pictures of five-elements theory, the earth element is always drawn in the middle. That is why Usagi is the leader, as her representation of earth makes her the center.

The pentagram shape of Usagi's transformation brooch in the second season has significance to it as well. This shape is featured in another notable part of the second season: it is the shape of the Crystal Palace, where Usagi will reign as Queen in the future. The logic behind creating the palace in the shape of a pentagram is actually quite sensible as a five-pointed palace offers far stronger fortification than other designs. From a Japanese historical perspective, it is interesting to note that there is precedence for such fortresses in Japan, like that of Hakodate in Hokkaido.[35]

The fortress at Hakodate.

Also important to the character's personalities is the consideration of blood type. There are various types of fortune telling in Japan, and one of the most popular is blood type divination. Blood type divination is considered a chic way to match up with your life partner, (roughly the equivalent of "what's your sign?" in the West), and some consider it serious enough to not date another based on blood incompatibility.

O blood types take risks and are leaders, have strong drives and often larger goals in mind. An A blood type means the person likes calm and peaceful relationships because they are very sensitive when there is something emotionally disturbing around. They are considerate but do not trust people easily, and are very strict in observing social norms. Blood types B have their own way of doing things and do not like it when people limit them. They are unconventional, do not care about social norms, and are fairly individualistic. Last are blood type ABs; their sense of critique is highly developed and they like to look at problems from a variety of angles. They want to contribute to their society even though they do not quite fit into it well.

As anyone who has seen *Sailor Moon* can attest, the characters' personalities fit with their blood type analyses. Usagi, her daughter Chibiusa, Makoto (Sailor Jupiter), and Michiru (Sailor Neptune) are all blood type O. The four of them all have strong leadership qualities. Mamoru (Tuxedo Mask), Ami (Sailor Mercury), and Setsuna (Sailor Pluto) are blood type A, and are the quietest characters in the series. Minako (Sailor Venus) and Haruka (Sailor Uranus) are blood type B, and both are extremely unique individuals. Rei (Sailor Mars) and Hotaru (Sailor Saturn) are blood types AB, and in the manga both are on the fringes of society.

Oriental astrology and blood type divination are cultural nuances that are integrated into the *Sailor Moon* universe. They are a part of the series that not many without special training or a particular interest in the fields would know about, and are thus just one of the many fantastic highlights that Takeuchi put into her work.

Venus Inside the Crescent Moon

Western mythology influences all the characters of the *Sailor Moon* universe, affecting everything from the characters' attacks to their physical appearance and even their attitudes towards love and life. Aside from Usagi Tsukino, Minako Aino's (Sailor Venus) life may be the most influenced by Western myth—and in her case, very ancient myth.

Ishtar and Selene / Venus and Moon

At a glance, Minako Aino is a clone of the series' heroine, Usagi Tsukino. The two are strikingly similar in appearance; with her hair down, Usagi is almost a dead ringer for Minako. Both also dislike studying and have a propensity to overeat and to be quite clumsy at times.

But Usagi and Minako are different characters. As opposed to the cowardly, clumsy crybaby Usagi, Minako started out as a rather rambunctious tomboy who was so boyish that her male classmates, at one point, wished they could see her cry, if only once. (To which Minako replied, "I never cry!") Minako is also a more mature type of person with many interests. In this way, the "twins" are almost polar opposites.

There are some similarities in their behavior. Usagi and Minako have similarly huge appetites, are always boy-chasing, and perform "stereo" actions (when they do things in the same manner simultaneously). Usagi and Minako do appear to have some kind of sisterly connection, as if they were separated from birth. It might, however, be more apt to say that the duo is cut from the same cloth. One often cited reason for the characters' similarities is that Takeuchi modeled Usagi after Minako when the *Sailor Moon* manga was given the green light for production. Takeuchi admits that Minako was her favorite character, so this is a reasonable conclusion. But we think there was more method to Takeuchi's choices. After all, it is one thing to duplicate Minako's personality in Usagi, but what about her appearance?

The phenomenon that does explain all these factors, providing an underpinning for their similar attitudes, close personal friendship, Venus' position as head of the four guardian sailor soldiers, and even her position as Usagi's decoy, is a deep mythological connection between the moon and Venus that stretches back thousands of years. A connection that, while something which would go right over the head of the uninformed Japanese viewer of the show, would leap out instantly to a Westerner relatively well versed in mythological study.

Ishtar and Venus

> "In ... ancient times, the Babylonian priest-astronomers devoted special attention to Ishtar [Venus] as a sister-star of the moon. [They watched] its appearances and disappearances with religious zest ..."[36]

While most readers easily associate Minako Aino and Sailor Venus with the Roman goddess Venus, many do not realize that the Venus myths (and their Greek counterparts through Aphrodite) trace their lineage even further back to the Babylonian Ishtar—goddess of love and war.

The Mark of Venus

One of Ishtar's most ancient symbols is a crescent of a rising new moon, a symbol of her in her guise as the Moon Goddess. Sailor V's primary "item" is the Crescent Moon Compact, which, as its name implies, is shaped like a crescent moon.

Moreover, the mark Sailor V wears on her head is a crescent moon turned upwards, just like on ancient statues of Ishtar. The upward crescent moon mark came to be the sign of the Moon Kingdom, but that was established when the *Sailor Moon* manga was created. Initially Minako was to be the lone heroine of *Sailor V*, so the upward crescent was most likely a mark of Venus as opposed to the moon.

The Crescent Moon Compact that Sailor V uses recharges under the light of a full moon. This is originally a pagan notion; many pagan rituals require wands and ceremonial items like crystals to be placed under a full moon in order to recharge. Even today the goddess Ishtar is worshipped by pagans, serving to further link Sailor V with Ishtar.

Other Venusian and Ishtarian symbolism involves Sailor V's Crescent Beam attack, which prominently features the confluence of two crescents. Ancient statues of Ishtar featured dual crescents on her head or garments. The crescents could refer to the crescent phases of Venus, or perhaps a combination of the lunar and Venusian crescents (symbolizing the moon and Venus together in the sky). The Holy Sword of the Moon as seen in the *Sailor Moon* manga also features dual crescents. Perhaps this, too, is symbolic of a Venus-Moon connection. Only Sailor Venus and Sailor Moon are ever able to wield the weapon properly.

She's Got the Power

Ishtar's mythological character is inextricably linked with both Venus and the moon, as is Minako's. While Ishtar is the embodiment of the goddess Venus, it is also said that "... as Queen of Heaven, she *replaced Sin as the moon deity* ... the zodiac was known as the 'girdle of Ishtar.'"[37] To the ancient Babylonians, the moon and Venus were both in positions of high esteem, considered far above the other planets:

> ... *It is quite clear that the [Babylonian] priests, watching for the moon's crescent, were struck by this most brilliant of stars [Venus] and that it must have appeared to them as an exceptional luminary. In later texts, Sun, Moon and Venus*

are often named together as a triad of related
deities, distinguished from the other four
[known] planets.[38]

Astronomically, there are more similarities between the two. Both Venus and the moon have phases (meaning Venus can be seen as a crescent at times), they are also often the only two bodies aside from the sun that can be seen in daylight, and they are also often seen quite close together in the sky. Is it any wonder that the characters of Venus and Moon would be closely linked, their avatars resembling one another?

Another fact elevates Aphrodite and Venus to a level akin to a monarch like Princess Serenity. The goddess Aphrodite was born before even *Zeus*, the king of the gods; she was formed from the remnants of Zeus' grandfather. In the *Sailor V* manga, it looks like this manner of birth was retained. Once, a character named Adonis showed Minako the "Venus Droplet," which had separated from the body of Princess Venus during her birth in the foamy seas of Venus.

The Lovely Goddess of Beauty and War

If Mars is the god of war, why is Venus the head of the Princess' guardians? Surprisingly, Ishtar was primarily a war goddess (the lioness of battle), but she also served the function of a goddess of love and justice. In *Sailor V* and *Sailor Moon*, Minako routinely refers to herself as a Soldier of "love and justice," so she certainly realized the dual nature of her role. And in an act of the *Sailor V* manga, Adonis, recalling Venus' past life, calls her "the lovely goddess of beauty and war."

In a First Dynasty Babylonian text, Ishtar is described as having a supreme position of respect and authority:

> *She is sought after among the Gods,*
> *extraordinary is her station. Respected is her*
> *word, it is supreme over them. Ishtar among the*
> *Gods, extraordinary is her station.*[39]

Similarly, in the manga, Sailor Venus is the head of the four "guardian soldiers" of the princess. She often devises some plan of action or leads them into battle. Immediately after appearing in the *Sailor Moon* manga, she assumes the mantle of authority and directs the others as to their course of action.

She is the one who arbitrarily decides the sailor soldiers must sacrifice their lives to stop the evil Metallia (a decision for which she is obeyed without question), and she is the one to ultimately wield the Holy Blade of the Mystical Silver Crystal (a parallel to Moon's ability to wield the Mystical Silver Crystal) and slay Queen Beryl.

Lover's Lament

Minako's love life (especially in the *Sailor V* manga) resonates almost perfectly with the love life of Ishtar, who has either killed or crippled the other males she has pursued. In the epic of *Gilgamesh*, Ishtar entreats Gilgamesh to become her husband, but Gilgamesh declines, citing her old lovers' fates:

> *"For Tamuz, the lover of thy youth,*
> *Thou has ordained wailing year after year.*
> *Having loved the dappled Shepherd-bird,*
> *Thou smotest him, breaking his wing.*
> ...
> *Then thou lovedst a lion, perfect in strength.*
> *Seven pits and seven didst thou dig for him.*
> *Then a stallion didst Thou love, famed in battle.*

The whip, the spur, the lash Thou ordainedst for him."[40]

While Minako's failed relationships with other men are not quite as intimate as her Babylonian counterpart's, the end result is no different. With rare exception (men like Alan and Asai who already have different girlfriends), the men Minako has dealt with have generally either ended up dead, wounded, or traumatized. The *Sailor V* manga even uses Minako's struggles as a gag in its ninth chapter, when Minako recites the laundry list of her past loves:

> *My first love, Higashi-senpai. But he died...* *(I killed him, sorta.)*
> *Gamer Taku. He was crazy... But I respect his skills at gaming.* [She beat him up rather badly without thinking.]
> ...
> *Saitou-senpai! But he seems rather violent.*

Saitou could be Dark Kingdom General Kunzite, an enemy in *Sailor Moon* whom Minako may have killed in her past life, and who she wounds in the anime. To this list we can add Officer Wakagi, whom she had a crush on (he was exiled to Siberia for quite some time as a result of his failure to catch Sailor V) and most poignant, Adonis, the man who has longed for her since his past life—and whom she kills (in self defense) after briefly falling in love with him.

Another parallel with Ishtar's love-life is the lack of a permanent male counterpart. Unlike Usagi, who has Mamoru, Minako always seems to be without a counterpart. Mythologically, Ishtar, too, was alone. It was said that her reign did not depend on a male consort, echoing Minako's words in the manga that "[she] didn't *need* boys." Of course, that didn't mean she wasn't *interested* in boys, just that her duty came first and that she was quite capable of surviving without them.

Minako the Destroyer

The Goddess Ishtar was also a goddess of death and destruction who was renowned for bringing down devastating deluges. Minako Aino shares these traits.

In one famous episode of *Sailor Moon*, Minako leaves a whimsical wake of devastation, destroying Rei Hino's stereo set, then spilling porridge all over her, and decimating the Tsukino household. During her career as Sailor V, Minako carved a swath of chaos and ruin throughout Tokyo as she foiled the dark ambitions of the Dark Agency.

Minako Aino is single-handedly responsible for the destruction of her friend Amano's apartment (blowing a hole in the side of the building), the *Este De Brine* building, and Avex Trax's Chinese studio, not to mention acts of petty vandalism (smashing in a steel door for no real reason and popping a motorcycle tire) and wanton negligence resulting in a full-scale gang war.

In the story of Minako and her mythological connections we see the power of reflective construction—just as we learn more about the mysteries and intricacies of Shinto via natural western curiosity about the exotic Rei's Hino's "job" as a miko, so too would curious Japanese viewers be able to access a veritable wealth of mythological, astrological and historical information just by investigating the lore behind her foreign-sounding, alter-ego name of "Venus."

<u>Conclusion</u>

Who Are These Warriors of Legend? — Revisited

On February 20, 1993, the first half of the *Sailor Moon* anime's original finale aired. In the episode, four of the sailor soldiers (Jupiter, Mercury, Venus and Mars) are consecutively hunted and murdered by the evil Dark Kingdom, whom they had been battling on television for nearly a year. Their on-screen deaths had traumatic consequences.

The episode ran at 7:00 p.m. on a Saturday, and many parents across Japan watched it with their children. That night and through the rest of the week, TV Asahi, which broadcast the program, was flooded with calls by concerned parents

TV Asahi, the station that broadcast
Sailor Moon in Japan.

whose children were crying. The parents demanded to know what would happen in the second half of the finale, to air the following week. One letter to the editor in a newspaper wrote that their nine-year-old child had started to cry during the episode and was so disturbed that she was unable to swallow food.

In another instance, a radio host, Arata Ōwada, said that she had become a fan of the show along with her child, and had sat down to watch the finale with her five-year old daughter.

Her daughter was so startled by the events of the final episodes that Ōwada had to call TV Asahi and ask them what was going to happen in the finale's conclusion to calm her daughter down. In a telephone interview with the magazine Animage (June 1993), Ōwada explained, "The finale was probably too much of a shock for my daughter. She missed a week of kindergarten with a high fever. When we went to the hospital, they told us that it was autotoxemia and asked if she endured any type of shock."[41]

To these children, the sailor soldiers were more than fictional characters. They were their friends; they referred to Usagi with affection as "Usagi-chan." (Adding "chan" to a name denotes familiarity.) Although the series was a fantasy, its characters so closely resembled real Japan that the loss of them in the series had an effect on the young viewers' psyche. When the second half of the finale aired the following week (created without the expectation that the show would continue), it included a segment after the trailer ensuring the audience that a second season was being prepared.

To the Japanese audience, this series was one that closely reflected their country and culture, with an added element of fantasy. Yet *Sailor Moon* has been one of Japan's most phenomenal global success stories of the recent decade. The cartoon version has aired in dozens of countries, in over fifteen languages, and on every continent but Antarctica. The themes that *Sailor Moon* imparts—loyalty, friendship, courage, love, are universal themes, that are understood and appreciated by children of every society. When the series is brought to another country, its Japanese elements fade into the background. Localized by language and often edited to make the characters appear as people from that country's society, the series' Japanese traits become sight-unseen.

Behind the localized façade lies *Sailor Moon*'s true

face. By better understanding who the sailor soldiers, our Warriors of Legend, really are, and what kind of city they live in, we have brought the generic back into the specific. We have found that *Sailor Moon* is a pop culture commodity that strongly depicts the society in which it was created. Although, as a commodity it can be changed to fit circumstance, it will always hold those reflections. Like Usagi bowing to a telephone pole, cultural references may go unnoticed by the viewer unfamiliar with how to interpret them. Once he or she is informed, however, rarely does it go unnoticed a second time. By understanding the nuances being depicted, the viewer better understands the society.

In this way, *Sailor Moon* can also be said to have prepared its viewers to better understand Japan. Its success has created a generation of children that have grown up having seen, but not interpreted, reflections of Japan. If, as we have done in this book, the background to interpret those reflections is provided, *Sailor Moon* and other pop culture products become more than entertainment. They are transformed into methods by which a foreign society's complexity, in this case that of Japan, may be better understood. *Sailor Moon* is one of many pop cultural ambassadors in this global age.

Footnotes

(1) Page 17 - Takeuchi, Naoko. *Princess Takeuchi Naoko's Return-to-Society Punch!!* Tokyo: Shueisha, 1999.

(2) 30 - Source: Demographia.com

(3) 31 - Source: http://www.city.minato.tokyo.jp/e/city/index.html

(4) 35 - Waley, Paul. *Tokyo: City of Stories.* New York: Weatherhill, 1991. Page 232.

(5) 36 - Bestor, Theodore. *Neighborhood Tokyo.* Stanford: Stanford University Press, 1989.

(6) 38 - Mitsunaka Tadano and Kenji Tokuda. *Sailormoon Speculate.*Tokyo: Kinema, 1994. Page 25.

(7) 40 - Japan Times. *Legacy of red-shoed girl lives on.* June 28, 2003.

(8) 43 - Mitsunaka Tadano and Kenji Tokuda. *Sailormoon Speculate.*Tokyo: Kinema, 1994. Page 32.

(9) 43 - Waley, Paul. *Tokyo Now and Then.* New York: Weatherhill, 1986.

(10) 47 - Mitsunaka Tadano and Kenji Tokuda. *Sailormoon Speculate.* Tokyo: Kinema, 1994. Pages 38-39.

(11) 48 - Waley, Paul. *Tokyo Now and Then.* New York: Weatherhill, 1986. Pages 390-391.

(12) 50 - Ibid, Pages 375-376.

(13) 52 - Waley, Paul. *Tokyo: City of Stories.* New York: Weatherhill, 1991

(14) 55 - Source: http://www.toyoeiwa.ac.jp/e_index.html

(15) 57 - Waley, Paul. *Tokyo Now and Then.* New York: Weatherhill, 1986. Pages 232-236.

(16) 58 - Mitsunaka Tadano and Kenji Tokuda. *Sailormoon Speculate.* Tokyo: Kinema, 1994. Pages 52-54.

(17) 59 - Ibid, Page 56.

(18) 61 - Ibid, Page 60.

(19) 63 - Ibid, Page 62.

(20) 64 - Waley, Paul. *Tokyo Now and Then.* New York: Weatherhill, 1986.

(21) 64 - Ai, Maeda. *Text and the City.* Duke University Press, 2004.

(22) 69 - Mitsunaka Tadano and Kenji Tokuda. *Sailormoon Speculate.* Tokyo: Kinema, 1994. Page 39.

(23) 69 - Bestor, Theodore. *Tsukiji: The Fish Market In the Center of the World.* Berkeley: University of California Press, 2004.

(24) 71 - Mitsunaka Tadano and Kenji Tokuda. *Sailormoon Speculate.* Tokyo: Kinema, 1994. Page 42.

(25) 74 - Sand, Jordan. *House and Home in Modern Japan.* Boston: Harvard

University Press, 2004.

(26) 76 - Juuban Irregulars. *Sailormoon no Himitsu*. Tokyo: Datahouse, 1993. Pages 63-64.

(27) 77 - Sand, Jordan. *House and Home in Modern Japan*. Boston: Harvard University Press, 2004.

(28) 99 - Juuban Irregulars. *Sailormoon no Himitsu*. Tokyo: Datahouse, 1993. Pages 65-66.

(29) 102 - Mitsunaka Tadano and Kenji Tokuda. *Sailormoon Speculate*. Tokyo: Kinema, 1994. Page 70.

(30) 110 - Robertson, Jennifer. *Takarazuka: Sexual Politics and Popular Culture in Japan*. Berkeley: University of California Press, 1998.

(31) 110 - Seidensticker, Edward. *Tokyo Rising*. New York: Knopf, 1990. Page 182.

(32) 119 - Littleton, C. Scott. *Shinto: Origins, Rituals, Festivals, Spirits, Sacred Places*. London: Oxford University Press, 2002.

(33) 124 - Juuban Irregulars. *Sailormoon R no Himitsu*. Tokyo: Datahouse, 1994. Pages 36-40.

(34) 127 - Hamilton, Edith. *Mythology*. New York: Warner books, 1999. Page 118.

(35) 133 - Mitsunaka Tadano and Kenji Tokuda. *Sailormoon Speculate*. Tokyo: Kinema, 1994. Pages 88-94.

(36) 136 - Pannekoek, A. *A History of Astronomy*. Dover Publishing, 1989. Page 35.

(37) 137 - themystica.org. Ishtar. Retrieved 12 June 2004 <http://www.themystica.org/mythical-folk/articles/ishtar.html>

(38) 138 - Pannekoek, A. *A History of Astronomy*. Dover Publishing, 1989. Page 35.

(39) 139 - Campanelli, Pauline. *Ishtar, In Her Praise, In Her Image*. Retrieved 16 June 2004 <http://www.paganlibrary.com/reference/ishtar-praise.php>

(40) 140 - Campanelli, Pauline. *Ishtar, In Her Praise, In Her Image*. Retrieved 16 June 2004 <http://www.paganlibrary.com/reference/ishtar-praise.php>

(41) 143 - Juuban Irregulars. *Sailormoon R no Himitsu*. Tokyo: Datahouse, 1994. Pages 95-96.

Acknowledgements

A book that has taken as many years to produce as this one does not get finished without the assistance of many individuals. Bruce Clark and Andrew Floyd provided immeasurable help, and sacrificed many hours to translating texts. Editor Jonathan Mays did an outstanding job transforming a vast array of project data into a cohesive, coherent whole, contributing a great deal of his own insight and knowledge to the text in the process. Hans Schumacher's cartographic skills and knowledge of the *Sailor Moon* world, as well as his many insights into the series, were invaluable. This book would not exist without them and is as much their book as our own.

From Columbia University, we thank Chad Diehl and Jonathan Twombly for reading and critiquing the book, as well as Professor Gregory M. Pflugfelder for advice and assistance. Jonathan went above and beyond the call of duty in practically copy editing the manuscript. We've tried to leave out the speculation and hope it is a little better than before.

Photographs come courtesy of Yosenex Orengo, who spent many hours running around Minato ward asking policemen for coffee shops and other places that disappeared a decade ago. Ian Miller and Jennifer Short's essays do not appear in this volume, but their work has not been for naught and will be in print in the future.

Last, and most of all, we must thank Naoko Takeuchi for the all the years and effort she put into crafting *Bishōjo Senshi Sailor Moon*. That this work could be based on what is, to most, a mere children's fantasy, is a testament to her skill in crafting such a finely detailed narrative; one rich in myth, legend, and fact.